What's Your
MAD ABOUT YOU
I.Q.?

D1706446

What's Your Mad About You I.Q.?

601 Questions and Answers for Fans

STEPHEN SPIGNESI

A CITADEL PRESS BOOK
Published by Carol Publishing Group

Frontispiece photo courtesy of Photofest.

A Citadel Press Book
Published by Carol Publishing Group
Citadel Press is a registered trademark of Carol Communications,
    Inc.
Editorial Offices: 600 Madison Avenue, New York, N.Y. 10022
Sales and Distribution Offices: 120 Enterprise Avenue, Secaucus,
    N.J. 07094
In Canada: Canadian Manda Group, One Atlantic Avenue, Suite 105,
    Toronto, Ontario M6K 3E7
Queries regarding rights and permissions should be addressed to
    Carol Publishing Group, 600 Madison Avenue, New York, N.Y. 10022

All photos unless otherwise indicated reproduced by permission
    of Photofest.

Carol Publishing Group books are available at special discounts for
bulk purchases, sales promotion, fund-raising, or educational
purposes. Special editions can be created to specifications. For
details, contact: Special Sales Department, Carol Publishing
Group, 120 Enterprise Avenue, Secaucus, N.J. 07094

MANUFACTURED IN THE UNITED STATES OF AMERICA

10   9   8   7   6   5   4   3   2   1

Library of Congress Cataloging-in-Publication Data

Spignesi, Stephen.
    What's your mad about you IQ? : 601 questions and answers for
fans / Stephen Spignesi.
        p.   cm.
    "A Citadel Press book."
    ISBN 0-8065-1682-8 (pbk.)
    1. Mad about you—Miscellanea.   I. Title.
PN1992.77.M22S65   1995
791.45'72—dc20   95-19777
                                                        CIP

**To
couplehood**

CONTENTS

Contents

ACKNOWLEDGMENTS

A multitude of thanks and much heartfelt gratitude to Steve Schragis, Hillel Black, John White, and *especially* George Beahm and Russell C. Friedberg, two stellar gentlemen without whom this book would not exist. Thanks, buds!

INTRODUCTION

MAD ABOUT MAD ABOUT YOU

> "Sometimes, after we've worked at something on stage for a week and a half, I go to my wife, 'Now! I have a snappy comeback! Say that again, what you said in July, go ahead! I'm ready now!'"
>
> —Paul Reiser, in *Entertainment Weekly*

ITEM: There is a MAD ABOUT YOU newsgroup on the Internet that has had thousands of postings about the show. One of these love letters from the fans specifically mentioned the episode "How to Fall in Love" in which Paul and Jamie are sitting in Riff's, and Helen Hunt's bare belly is briefly visible. Ahah, I thought: Here comes something cyberspatially salacious. But no, the "poster" concluded his discussion of the scene in question with something along the lines of "Is Helen Hunt the cutest thing you've ever seen or what!?" Paul, Helen, and MAD ABOUT YOU have that effect on people.

In New York City, in an apartment building on the corner of Twelfth Street and Fifth Avenue, there lives a young couple named Paul and Jamie Buchman.

Paul and Jamie have been married for three years or so,

and they've been together as a couple longer than that. They have a dog named Murray and a fascinating collection of assorted friends and relatives who enrich and complicate their lives.

Paul and Jamie share their life with us every week in a wonderful television show called *Mad About You.*

And ever since the show premiered back in September of 1992, the number of its fans has grown enormously.

What's Your Mad About You *I.Q.?* quizzes you on your knowledge of the goings-on in that Big Apple apartment and the events in the lives of Paul and Jamie Buchman, as well as the antics of Lisa, Ira, Fran, Paul and Jamie's parents, and the many other weird and wonderful characters who drift in and out of their (and our!) lives every Thursday night.

Start with "The Basics" and work your way through all your beloved characters and favorite moments from the show. Take the *Mad About You* Word Search Puzzle.

Have fun with the Buchmans.

And then have a glass of guava juice. You do know, don't you, that guava is as much fun to say as it is to drink?

I thought so.

THE *MAD ABOUT YOU* GRADING SYSTEM

What's Your Mad About You *I.Q.?* consists of 601 questions organized into chapters ranging from "The Basics" and "Paul and Jamie Buchman," to "Food," "Work," and "Guest Stars."

This Grading System will tell you where you score, beginning with the not-too-swift *Murray "Good Boy" Medal* and peaking with the ultimate *Jamie Buchman Achievement Award.*

Number of Correct Answers	*The* Mad About You *Award*
0-100	**THE MURRAY "GOOD BOY" MEDAL:** You are a human being with Murrayness! Get the mouse!
101-200	**THE URSULA THE WAITRESS "GOLDEN SPOON" AWARD:** Sorry, but you are as clueless as a human person can be without being Murray!
201-300	**THE LISA DYSFUNCTIONALITY TROPHY:** Well, duh?
301-400	**THE GUS STEMPLE "IT'S A FACT!" AWARD:** As "well done" as barbecued ribs!
401-500	**THE PAUL BUCHMAN "SILVER SPROCKET" AWARD:** Hello? How do you know this?!
501-601	**THE JAMIE BUCHMAN ACHIEVEMENT AWARD:** I love how you know things!

Mad About You: The Basics

A typical morning in the Buchman apartment, with Paul and
Jamie fighting for mirror space.

This chapter tests your knowledge of *Mad About You* fundamentals, including Jamie and Paul's two dry cleaners and who, exactly, is Koko, anyway?

1 Name the holiday on which Paul and Jamie moved into the apartment together.

    A. Halloween

    B. New Year's Day

    C. President's Day

    D. Valentine's Day

2 On what day of the week was *Mad About You* broadcast in its first season?

    A. Sunday

    B. Monday

    C. Wednesday

    D. Thursday

3 TRUE OR FALSE: Jamie never remembered to enter the ATM withdrawals in the checkbook so the Buchmans were always sixty dollars off.

4 What was *Mad About You*'s first time slot?

    A. 8:00 P.M.

    B. 8:30 P.M.

    C. 9:00 P.M.

    D. 9:30 P.M.

5 Which *Mad About You* characters *other* than Paul and Jamie Buchman have appeared in *every* episode of the series?

    A. Murray

    B. Ira

    C. Fran and Mark

    D. Lisa

    E. Paul and Jamie are the only characters who have appeared in every single episode.

6 TRUE OR FALSE: Jamie and Paul have two gay friends named Eddie and Rob.

7 What was Paul and Jamie's wedding song?

    A. "Endless Love"

    B. "Color My World"

    C. "Love Is a Many-Splendored Thing"

    D. "Play That Funky Music, White Boy"

8 When Paul and Jamie made out their wills, they decided who would get what. Match these two "assets" with their appropriate "heir."

    A. Paul's stereo   1. Lisa

    B. Jamie's couch   2. Selby

9 When they made out their wills, whom did Jamie designate with Power of Attorney?

    A. Her mother Theresa

    B. Fran

C. Her sister Lisa
D. Her father Gus

10 What are the names of the two dry cleaners Paul and Jamie used?

A. A & A Cleaners
B. Lumberto's
C. Pedro's
D. Snappy Garments

11 TRUE OR FALSE: Before they "officially" met, Paul pretended he was Jamie's houseboy Koko in order to find out where she worked.

12 Acting on Jamie and Fran's orders, Mark quizzed Paul about certain aspects of his life. Supply Paul's answers (paraphrases are okay!) to the following five rapid-fire questions Mark asked him:

A. How much money do you make?
B. Own or rent?
C. Previous marriages?
D. Smoker?
E. Drinker?

13 When was the very first time Jamie ever called Paul "Honey"?

14 What is the name of Jamie's hairdresser?

A. Darryl
B. Harold
C. Lloyd

15 Where did Paul and Jamie store their wedding album?

    A. Behind the toilet

    B. Under the bed

    C. In the living room closet with their "personal" home video

    D. In the refrigerator

16 FILL IN THE BLANKS: Paul had two sisters, _____ and _____ .

17 What was Paul and Jamie's bank?

    A. First Bank of Manhattan

    B. Second Bank of New York

    C. Citibank

18 What was the name of Paul and Jamie's "cleaning genie"?

    A. Jabar

    B. Raoul

    C. Willie

19 TRUE OR FALSE: Paul and Jamie's pharmacist's name is Schultz.

20 Paul and Jamie belonged to a certain "_____ of the Month" club. What commodity did they have delivered every month?

    A. Wine

    B. Meat

    C. Bread

    D. Fruit

21 Where did Paul and Jamie keep their passports?
  A. In the cabinet above the refrigerator.
  B. In a bank safe deposit box.
  C. In Paul's sock drawer.

For Seriously *Mad* Fans

22 What was the address of the apartment where Paul was living when he met Jamie?
  A. 125 East 81st
  B. 104 East 63rd
  C. 129 West 81st

23 What was the address of the apartment where Jamie lived before moving in with Paul?
  A. 125 East 81st
  B. 104 East 63rd
  C. 142 West 81st

The "History of a Buchman" Question

24 I, your author, was born and raised in New Haven, Connecticut. Why am I telling you this in a book about *Mad About You?*

Morbidly *Mad*

25 What did Paul and Jamie's first meeting and their train ride to Connecticut for Thanksgiving have in common? (HINT: Think "death.")

2

Jamie and Paul Buchman

Paul and Jamie during a fateful trip to the Museum of Natural History.

How much do you know about our favorite married couple?

Jamie

26 From what university did Jamie graduate?
- A. Yale
- B. Harvard
- C. NYU
- D. Columbia

27 TRUE OR FALSE: Jamie snores.

28 What was the title of Jamie's failed college novel?
- A. *New Haven*
- B. *My Sister, My Self*
- C. *Crying in the Rain*

29 TRUE OR FALSE: Jamie wants to be cremated.

30 What famous tennis pro did Jamie choose to "interact with" for her "virtual reality" experience?
- A. Andre Agassi
- B. John McEnroe
- C. Yannick Noah

31 TRICK QUESTION: What is Jamie's *real* middle name?

32 According to Jamie, what British author makes her hot?

    A. Jane Austen

    B. Charles Dickens

    C. William Blake

33 How many majors did Jamie pursue during her college years?

    A. One

    B. Two

    C. Three

    D. Four

34 What was the name of the nonexistent "biker bar" Jamie said she used to hang around in order to make an impression in Paul's fifteen-minute documentary?

    A. Bikes 'n' Things

    B. Bikes R Us

    C. Bikes 'n' More

35 TRUE OR FALSE: Jamie has family in Israel.

36 What shape is Jamie's face?

    A. Octagonal

    B. Round

    C. Trapezoidal

37 When Jamie went back to school after she quit her PR job, she initially took four courses. Which of the following courses did she sign up for?

    • Ethics

    • Philosophy

- Psychology
- Logic
- Chemistry
- American Literature
- Intermediate French
- Statistics

38 What specific body part of Jamie's "virtual reality" tennis pro did she admit she was quite fond of?

A. His chest
B. His butt
C. His feet
D. His legs

39 In the book she wrote about some of her patients, what pseudonym did Lisa's shrink use for Jamie?

A. Maria
B. Stella
C. Eunice

40 What was Jamie's "job" at Camp Winiwaug?

A. She was a cafeteria worker.
B. She was a lifeguard.
C. She was a bunk monitor.
D. She was a camp counselor.

41 What did Jamie's old boyfriend Sherman Williams do for a living?

A. He was a football player.
B. He was an aerobics instructor.
C. He was a house painter.

42 What was Jamie's dark secret that Paul weaseled out of her at a wedding?

A. Her real name was Henrietta.

B. Two weeks before she and Paul moved in together, she had a date with a guy she worked with and had sex with him.

C. She regularly used Paul's razor to shave her legs and then lied about it to him.

43 TRUE OR FALSE: Jamie once dated a poet named Monroe.

44 What was the name of Jamie's ex-boyfriend whom Paul called a "pituitary case" and who Jamie claimed could snap Paul "like a twig"? (HINT: "football shirt")

A. Lloyd

B. Hasten

C. Billington

D. Alan

45 What instrument did Jamie play in her high school orchestra?

A. Clarinet

B. Cello

C. Saxophone

D. Trombone

46 TRUE OR FALSE: Jamie once spent three weeks in a convent.

47 Which Carrie Fisher novel was Jamie seen reading on the train ride home from Thanksgiving with her family?

    A. *Delusions of Grandma*

    B. *Postcards From the Edge*

    C. *Surrender the Pink*

48 TRUE OR FALSE: According to Lisa, the reason why Billy Slater loved Jamie was that she once showed him her boobs.

49 How many boyfriends did Jamie have during her college years?

    A. Five

    B. Six

    C. Seven

    D. Eight

50 TRUE OR FALSE: Jamie has a tattoo.

51 In what high school musical did Jamie's former fiancé Hap Evans play the lead?

    A. *Oklahoma!*

    B. *South Pacific*

    C. *The Music Man*

    D. *My Fair Lady*

52 Which of Jamie's old boyfriends became a congressman?

    A. Alan

    B. Sherman

    C. Stan

    D. Arnold

For Extremely Serious "Jamie Buchman" Fans

53 What time was Jamie Stemple born?

54 How many teeth does Jamie have?
   A. Twenty-nine
   B. Thirty-one
   C. Thirty-two

55 Which of the following symbols did Jamie use in her electronic journal to rate her sexual encounters?
   A. Hearts
   B. Balloons
   C. Stars
   D. Smiley faces

Paul

56 TRUE OR FALSE: Paul owned a Volvo.

57 Which of the following comedy teams is a favorite of Paul's? (We learned this in an episode involving a particularly traumatic haircut!)
   A. The Marx Brothers
   B. Abbott and Costello
   C. Laurel and Hardy
   D. The Three Stooges

58 TRUE OR FALSE: Paul loved riding backwards on trains.

59 What is the one mode of transportation Paul never uses?

    A. Subway

    B. Cab

    C. Bus

    D. Bicycle

60 TRUE OR FALSE: Generally, Paul never wore cologne.

61 What famous supermodel did Paul choose to "interact with" for his "virtual reality" experience?

    A. Elle MacPherson

    B. Claudia Shiffer

    C. Christie Brinkley

62 TRUE OR FALSE: Paul once wrote an entire book of poems for Lynne Stoddard.

63 What was Paul doing that Jamie described as "stacking, arranging, aligning, adjusting, annoying"?

64 TRUE OR FALSE: Paul has capped teeth.

65 A number performed by a famous country singer accompanied Paul's precognitive "big fat globs floating around" dream. Name this singer. (HINT: The song he heard in his dream was "Crazy.")

    A. Reba McEntire

    B. Dolly Parton

    C. Patsy Cline

66 What famous serial killer and cannibal did Paul once think Jamie looked like?

67 What were the two things Paul said he never liked to lend?
   A. His books and his CDs
   B. His cream cheese and his electric razor
   C. His clothes and his collection of baseball caps
   D. Money and his internal organs

68 TRUE OR FALSE: Paul loves opera.

69 TRUE OR FALSE: Paul liked his shower "light and gentle."

70 What was Paul's shoe size?
   A. 9 E
   B. 9½ D
   C. 8 D
   D. 8½ D

71 What happened to Paul's ears when he got turned on?

72 TRUE OR FALSE: Paul was once mistaken for Wayne Rogers and then yelled at for leaving *M*A*S*H*.

73 What was Paul's former film classmate Howie Balenger doing for a living when Paul ran into him years after they were in school together?
   A. He was a New York subway token clerk.
   B. He was a pretzel vendor.

C. He was a priest.

D. He was a mounted police officer.

74 TRUE OR FALSE: Paul whines in his sleep.

75 What film school did Paul attend?

A. Columbia Film School

B. SUNY Albany Film School

C. New York University (NYU) Film School

D. Yale Drama School

76 FILL IN THE BLANK: Paul once rented an adult movie called *Pumping* _____ that he tried to persuade Jamie he should be able to deduct as a business expense.

77 What happened to Paul's testicles when he and Jamie went for a dawn Polar Bear Swim during their weekend in Vermont?

78 TRUE OR FALSE: In 1980, Paul was voted Most Promising Filmmaker at his film school.

79 What pseudonym did Lisa's shrink use for Paul in the book she wrote about some of her patients?

A. Larry

B. Raoul

C. David

80 TRUE OR FALSE: Paul once won a National Endowment for the Arts grant.

81 As a child, Paul was once tormented by the Escobar brothers (Matty, Felipé, and Jesus) on Halloween. What was Paul's costume the year the Escobar boys threw candy corn at him?

    A. Batman

    B. Superman

    C. Spiderman

    D. Darth Vader

82 TRUE OR FALSE: Paul snored through *Les Miz* (*Les Miserables*).

83 TRUE OR FALSE: Paul once said he would love to be married to someone named "Uma" so that every morning he could call out, "Uma, eggs!"

84 What ice cream-related occupation did Paul say he'd choose if he could have any job he wanted?

85 TRUE OR FALSE: Paul had leopard print bikini underwear that made him feel "special."

86 TRUE OR FALSE: Paul had clogged pores.

87 What side of the bed does Paul sleep on?

The Happy Couple

88 Where did Paul and Jamie first kiss?

    A. In Fran's office during a Christmas party.

    B. At the Rockefeller Plaza ice-skating rink.

    C. At a newsstand.

89 When Jamie caught Paul in the tub with all their wedding "Thank You" notes in the water, what soap company did he tell her he was writing to in order to get out of trouble?

    A. Dove

    B. Ivory

    C. Zest

    D. Dial

90 What was Paul and Jamie's "get me away from this boring person" signal?

    A. They would run their hands through their hair.

    B. They would use the word "paramecium" in a sentence.

    C. They would ask, "How was the scrod?"

91 When Paul and Jamie were imprisoned in their bathroom on Valentine's Day, Jamie made Paul stand in the tub and sing while she peed. From what musical did Paul sing a selection?

    A. *Brigadoon*

    B. *The Music Man*

    C. *The King and I*

92 What was the name of the Vermont inn where Paul and Jamie attempted their "weekend getaway"?

    A. The Babcock Inn

    B. The Conrad Inn

    C. The Hartley Lodge

93 Which of the following phone numbers did Jamie leave for Lisa when she and Paul went away to Vermont for the weekend?

    A. Their doctor

    B. The neighborhood watch

    C. Murray's vet

    D. All of the above

94 What football player did Paul say Jamie's boss's wife looked like?

    A. Joe Namath

    B. Don Shula

    C. O. J. Simpson

    D. Refrigerator Perry

95 Jamie once bought a vacuum hair cutting machine that was known as the "Ginsu knife of hairstyling." What was the name of this product?

    A. The Vacu-Trim II

    B. The Suck-Cut Deluxe

    C. The Air-Cut Hair-Cut

96 What specific dental hygiene practice of Jamie's consistently aggravated Paul? (HINT: Think "waxed" or "unwaxed.")

97 FILL IN THE BLANK: When Jamie decided to go back to school after quitting her PR job, Paul stupidly forgot to mail in her _____ .

98 Through the end of the third season, exactly how many times had Paul and Jamie had sex on their kitchen table when there were other people in the apartment?

99 What was the only television show that could be watched at the Vermont inn Paul and Jamie visited during their "weekend getaway"?

    A. *Columbo*

    B. *Barnaby Jones*

    C. *The Big Valley*

    D. *Baywatch*

100 Paul and Jamie once had a famous New York restaurant all to themselves, thanks to the generosity of billionaire Freddy Statler. What restaurant did Statler reserve just for the two of them?

    A. The Rainbow Room

    B. The Four Seasons

    C. The Russian Tea Room

    D. Lutecé

101 Paul and Jamie once signed a guest book "Leonard and Donna." Where were they when they used these phony names?

102 What one specific wedding picture did Paul and Jamie *not* have in their wedding album?

    A. The "feeding each other cake" picture

    B. The "tossing the bouquet" picture

    C. The "putting on the garter" picture

    D. The "leaving for the honeymoon" picture

103 What was Paul talking about when he told Jamie, "It makes me look rugged"?

    A. His new Gore-Tex parka

    B. His new beard

    C. His "muscle" T-shirt

    D. His new wire-rimmed glasses

104 Where did Jamie get her "strong admiring wife thing" in the first place?

105 Instead of returning a movie he had rented, Paul accidentally gave the video store his and Jamie's homemade porno tape. What movie did he *mean* to return?

    A. *Son of Paleface*

    B. *Robocop 2*

    C. *The Silence of the Lambs*

106 What was the name of the flirtatious twenty-five-year-old male college student whom Paul had to politely (sort of) tell not to touch Jamie?

    A. Nick

    B. Dick

    C. Rick

A *Mad About You* "Classic Moments" Question

107 While having phone sex, Jamie responded to one of Paul's endearments with, "What niece? I don't have a niece!" What in the world could Paul have said during *phone sex* to elicit that response from Jamie?

Jamie and Paul Buchman

A "Think Carefully" True Or False

108 The first time Paul and Jamie ever met was at a newsstand when they both wanted the last copy of the *New York Times*.

11D

The Apartment

3

◀

Paul, Jamie, and wacky billionaire Freddy Statler
(Jerry Lewis).

Questions about the place Paul and Jamie call home.

Home Sweet Home: Apartment 11D

109 How many times did Paul and Jamie look at the apartment before they decided to rent it?

    A. Twice

    B. Four times

    C. Six times

110 What specific floor flaw in the apartment (which Paul steadfastly refused to admit even existed) continually annoyed Jamie?

111 TRUE OR FALSE: In the special, one-hour "wedding" episode, Paul and Jamie cleaned out the freezer in their apartment, initially throwing out three things: a bag of frozen vegetables, the top of their wedding cake, and a fish Jamie's father caught. Ultimately, only the fish remained in the trash.

112 Who lived in Paul and Jamie's apartment before they moved in?

    A. A chiropractor and his male companion

    B. An electrical engineer and his wife

    C. Three female college roommates

    D. The mayor's personal assistant

113 After working together all day on a commercial, Paul and Jamie couldn't stand being together in the apartment and thus welcomed a call from the Time-Life operator. What did the operator want to sell them?

    A. The *Gunslingers of the Old West* series

    B. The *True Crime* series

    C. The *Mysteries of the Supernatural* series

    D. A subscription to *Time* magazine

114 Where in the apartment did Jamie and Paul keep their fire extinguisher?

    A. In the living room closet

    B. In the bathroom vanity

    C. Under the sink

    D. In the bedroom closet

115 Certain appliance combinations always popped circuit breakers in the Buchman's apartment. From the following four devices, match the two pairs that always blew the breaker:

    A. Blender

    B. Toaster

    C. Blow dryer

    D. Popcorn maker

116 What X-rated cable channel did Paul and Jamie get in their apartment after Jamie illegally hooked up the bedroom set?

    A. The Spice Channel

    B. The Blue Channel

C. The Playboy Channel
D. Exotica

117 TRUE OR FALSE: The apartment in Sylvia's building that she wanted Jamie and Paul to move into included utilities in the rent.

118 What "completely out of character" magazine did Paul and Jamie place on their apartment coffee table for Paul's fifteen-minute documentary?
A. *Bon Appetit*
B. *Civil War Journal*
C. *Scientific American*

119 Where in the Buchmans' apartment did Mr. Wicker find the packet of wartime letters of Millie and Leo?
A. Under a floor board
B. Behind the toilet
C. In a closet

120 Jamie's movers couldn't squeeze an armoire through the apartment door because she mistakenly read 39 inches as 34 inches. What was the width of the Buchmans' apartment door?

121 There was one specific bathroom chore for which Paul never seemed to take responsibility, a failing that once drove a fuming Jamie to come into the living room and give him a demonstration of how to do it. What was this hygiene-related chore?
A. Putting the cap back on the toothpaste tube.
B. Cleaning the hair out of the tub drain.
C. Putting a new roll of toilet paper in the holder.

122 What musical instrument do Paul and Jamie have in their apartment bedroom?

    A. A guitar

    B. A saxophone

    C. A piano

The Buchmans' Building: 51 Fifth Avenue

123 Which of their neighbors was Paul talking about when he admitted that he and Jamie had almost killed them, fondled their underwear, and violated their livestock? (The Buchmans gave them poison pizza; Paul put her panties on his head; and Murray impregnated their dog.)

124 Other than Eddie, there was at least one other doorman at the Buchmans' building. Who was it?

125 TRUE OR FALSE: Paul and Jamie's front door had a peephole.

126 Paul and Jamie's neighbors, the Hamiltons, had a particularly annoying poster on the front door of their apartment which the Buchmans stole one day. What was it?

    A. A peace symbol

    B. A happy face

    C. A Santa Claus

127 Who was the elevator operator in the Buchmans' building?

    A. Mr. Wicker

    B. Eddie

C. Lou

D. José

128 What type of footwear did the Buchmans give Mr. Wicker for Christmas one year?

A. Slippers

B. Running shoes

C. Totes

129 Who are "The Sconeheads"?

130 Which of the following "services" did Mr. Wicker perform for Annabelle Stern in 11J, much to Mrs. Wicker's dismay?

A. He unbended her venetian blinds.

B. He Rustoleumed her fire escape.

C. He fixed her toaster.

D. All of the above.

131 TRUE OR FALSE: Paul and Jamie's landlord was Mr. Wicker.

132 TRUE OR FALSE: Paul and Jamie live on Manhattan's Upper West Side.

133 What course did Hal Conway, Paul and Jamie's neighbor across the hall, teach at Columbia?

A. Economics

B. Physics

C. Ethics

D. Diplomacy

134 The Cohens in 12K had a cat named Admiral Cheswick who repeatedly did something unpleasant in the building's elevator. What did Cheswick do?

    A. He peed in the elevator.

    B. He scratched the wallpaper off the wall.

    C. He hissed and spit whenever someone else got on the elevator.

135 TRUE OR FALSE: When Mr. Wicker moved in with the Buchmans, he and his wife had been married for forty years.

136 TRUE OR FALSE: Jamie never did laundry between four and six because she didn't want to run into the Kopeks. (Paul and Jamie didn't like them.)

137 Mrs. Wicker once did a commercial for an over-the-counter cold remedy. What was it?

    A. Dristan

    B. Sudafed

    C. Contac

    D. Nyquil

138 TRUE OR FALSE: Mrs. Wicker was once nominated for a Cleo Award for her commercial work.

The Neighborhood: A "Krazy About Kim" Question

139 Paul and Jamie's favorite neighborhood market was owned and operated by an Asian named Kim, who had the tendency to speak in series of three nouns at a time (give or take the occasional compound noun). In the hour-long episode "With This Ring" (the second season finale), Kim outdoes himself with five fascinating triples. In the following table, complete Kim's trio with a noun from the second column:

1. "We've cakes, we've Drano, we've _____ by the pound."	A. "Q-Tips" B. "Aspergum and Yodels"
2. "We've beer, we've _____ , we've lemon pie."	C. "Pepto"
3. "We've sugar, we've onions, we've _____ ."	D. "wife"
4. "We've _____ , we've Bromo, we've Alka-Seltzer."	E. "cheese"
5. "I've a market, I've a _____ , I've a daughter."	

An "Are You Paying Attention?" True or False

140 Paul and Jamie's neighbors in 9D once gave out Bosnian relief donation certificates for Halloween.

For Seriously *Mad* Fans

141 One of Paul and Jamie's neighbors was Harrison Delahanty, who was on the board of an organization from which Paul was seeking a grant, and who lived in apartment 3G. What kind of maintenance problems did Mr. Wicker tell the Buchmans Mr. Delahanty had?

A. "Toilet troubles like you wouldn't believe."
B. "Bad switches. Really bad switches."
C. "Big radiator problems."
D. "Linoleum bubbles. It's not a pretty sight."

(PHOTOFEST)

4

A Mad About You Miscellany

◀

The 1992 cast of *Mad About You*. Left to right: Tommy Hinkley (Jay Selby), Anne Ramsay (Lisa Stemple), Paul Reiser (Paul Buchman), Leila Kenzel (Fran Devanow), and Richard Kind (Mark Devanow).

This chapter quizzes you on miscellaneous, fun *Mad About You* trivia and goings-on.

142 While sitting in Riff's one day, Jamie and Fran each picked three male celebrities they would love to sleep with. From the following stars, identify who picked whom:

    A. John Goodman
    B. Mick Jagger
    C. Yannick Noah
    D. Bruce Springsteen
    E. Joe Namath
    F. Tom Brokaw

143 To kill time during her first (disastrous) Thanksgiving dinner party, Jamie made everyone sit in a circle and tell what they were thankful for. From the following list, match the person with what they said they were thankful for:

    1. Burt   A. That they'd be eating soon.
    2. Gus   B. Chuckles (the candy).
    3. Lisa   C. An alphabetical list from "Apple
    4. Ira   Blossom Time" to "Vinyl."
    5. Jamie D. Therapy tomorrow.
               E. A parking space with no meter.

The "Spy Girl" Section

144 On what day of the week did *Spy Girl* air? (HINT: Possibly *Home Improvement*'s slot?)
- A. Monday
- B. Tuesday
- C. Wednesday

145 For how many years was *Spy Girl* on the air? (HINT: It was a *very* successful show.)
- A. Two
- B. Four
- C. Six

146 Spy Girl's nefarious nemesis organization was called SCRUM, which stood for the Society for the _____ and _____ of Universal Mankind.

147 Paul and Ira both collected *Spy Girl* memorabilia when they were kids. For the following six *Spy Girl* items, tell whether Paul or Ira owned it:
- A. *Spy Girl* Thermos
- B. *Spy Girl* Action Set
- C. *Spy Girl* Lunch Box
- D. *Spy Girl* Doll
- E. *Spy Girl* Badge
- F. *Spy Girl* Walkie-Talkies

148 TRUE OR FALSE: Diane "Spy Girl" Caldwell had an affair with Adam "Batman" West.

149 What was the title of Diane Caldwell's autobiography?

   A. *Spy Girl Uncovered*

   B. *I, Spy Girl*

   C. *Spy Girl Lives!*

Music and Musicals

150 On whose album cover was Jamie's ex-boyfriend Alan the artist working when Jamie ran into him at one of Fran's parties?

   A. Sting

   B. Phil Collins

   C. Peter Gabriel

151 In which of the following theatrical productions did Diane "Spy Girl" Caldwell appear after *Spy Girl* went off the air?

   A. *Brigadoon*

   B. *King Lear*

   C. *Plaza Suite*

   D. All of the above

152 TRUE OR FALSE: The guy who got into Paul and Jamie's cab the night they met Velma was going to see *Les Miserables*.

153 What was the name of the CD of wartime music that Jamie bought at Tower Records?

   A. *Dancing Through World War II*

   B. *"I'll Be Seeing You" & Other World War II Hits*

   C. *Great Songs of World War II*

154 TRUE OR FALSE: Twenty years after high school, Ira's "wife" Marianne still had Paul's Pink Floyd albums.

155 What famous country music star identified a song for Paul and Jamie at Riff's?

    A. Mel Tillis

    B. Garth Brooks

    C. Reba McEntire

    D. Alan Jackson

156 What Broadway musical did Paul plan on taking Jamie to see for her thirtieth birthday?

    A. *The Phantom of the Opera*

    B. *Tommy*

    C. *Miss Saigon*

    D. *Cats*

157 A singer named Loretta once auditioned for Paul by leaving twenty minutes from a certain musical on his answering machine. Name this musical.

    A. *The Phantom of the Opera*

    B. *Cats*

    C. *Miss Saigon*

    D. *South Pacific*

158 FILL IN THE BLANK: When an optical store clerk told Paul he had "classical" features, he replied, "I always thought I had _____ features."

159 During what opera did Jamie and her ex-boyfriend Alan have a big fight?

    A. *Aida*

    B. *The Marriage of Figaro*

    C. *La Traviata*

160 TRUE OR FALSE: Lisa and Jamie did *Pippin* in high school and Lisa was the loudest one in the chorus.

A Few Movie Questions

161 On which Bob Hope movie did Paul rack up $38 in late charges at Video Vogue (and which he could have bought for $6.99)?

    A. *My Favorite Blonde*

    B. *The Paleface*

    C. *Son of Paleface*

162 While trying to "pick up" Jamie as research for a documentary he was making about dating, Paul told her he looked like a certain actor in a certain movie. Name him.

    A. Ray Liotta in *GoodFellas*

    B. Kevin Costner in *The Bodyguard*

    C. Patrick Swayze in *Ghost*

    D. Daniel Day-Lewis in *The Last of the Mohicans*

163 Before Paul and Jamie went to see the "feelgood movie of the year" with Ira and his new date, Jamie bought Marilyn's daughter a gift from a street vendor. What did she buy the young college student? (HINT: The guy threw in a bag of tangerines and a pair of thigh-highs.)

    A. A dictionary

    B. A fake Rolex

    C. A briefcase

164 Who produced *Casablanca*?

165 TRUE OR FALSE: Paul had a video of *West Side Story*.

166 What movie starring Mickey Rourke, Eric Roberts, and Daryl Hannah did Paul once recommend to the clerk at the Video Vogue? (HINT: "Pauly, they took my thumb!")

167 What is the name of Paul and Jamie's favorite clerk at Video Vogue? (HINT: He looks like Larry of The Three Stooges.)
   A. Dutch
   B. Spike
   C. Lloyd

168 What was the name of the British miniseries that Paul wanted to watch and that Jamie accidentally taped over with a supermarket shopping show?
   A. *Ten Steps to Lancashire*
   B. *The Upstairs Maid*
   C. *The Barrister in the Bog*
   D. *The Best Interests of Eleanor*

169 FILL IN THE BLANK: In order to retrieve their home-made porno tape from Roy Osterback, Jamie pretended she was doing a "video recall" for the FCC. To get him to give up the tape she told Roy that it was one of the new "_____-based tapes."
   A. Fluoride
   B. Chloride
   C. Chlorine
   D. Magnesium

170 What Katharine Hepburn movie did Paul mention when he saw Jamie dressed in her "anti-sun" sunbathing dress, hat, and scarf?

    A. *The Lion in Winter*

    B. *On Golden Pond*

    C. *The African Queen*

Books and Magazine Mania

171 In what magazine did Jamie read the article "Sleeping Habits of the Stars" in which she learned that Tony Randall took naps?

    A. *Cosmopolitan*

    B. *Vogue*

    C. *Vanity Fair*

172 After quitting her job, Jamie talked about reading the complete works of which classic woman writer?

    A. Eudora Welty

    B. Virginia Woolf

    C. Jane Austen

    D. Sylvia Plath

173 According to Jamie, what were the only two periodicals she and Paul actually read?

    A. *TV Guide* and the *Victoria's Secret* catalog

    B. *Time* and the *National Enquirer*

    C. *TV Guide* and the *Star*

174 What magazine did Jamie find under Paul's mattress when they stayed at his parents' apartment when Burt was in the hospital?

    A. *Penthouse*

    B. *Hustler*

    C. *Gent*

    D. *Playboy*

175 What byline did Jamie use for a short story she was planning on submitting around the time Mr. Wicker found the "love letters"?

    A. Jamie Stemple Buchman

    B. J. S. Buchman

    C. Jamie S. Buchman

    D. Jamie Stemple

Totally Tubular

176 What *extremely p*opular television show known for its gorgeous women did Paul one day admit taping?

    A. *Melrose Place*

    B. *Baywatch*

    C. *Beverly Hills 90210*

177 What television show did Jamie accidentally tape over *Casablanca*?

    A. The *Baywatch* Christmas special

    B. "Gay Pets Mourn Their Lost Lovers: A Very Special *Geraldo*"

    C. "Today on *Oprah*: Hookers Predict the Oscars!"

    D. Four hours of jewelry on the Home Shopping Club

178 When Paul yelled out the window at a loud neighbor that he was trying to make love to his wife, the neighbor yelled back, "I *already* made love to your wife." What sitcom character did Jamie tell Paul he was acting like by shouting out the window in such a manner?

A. Ricky Ricardo
B. Ralph Kramden
C. Barney Fife
D. Al Bundy

179 Paul considerately gave Masha the maid videotapes of her favorite sitcom. Of what show was Masha (appropriately) a big fan?

A. *Bewitched*
B. *I Love Lucy*
C. *Hazel*
D. *The Brady Bunch*

"Also Known As . . ." Section

180 Who is "Pedro the Cabana Boy"?

181 Who are "Queen Love Bug" and the "Love Bug King"?

182 Who are "Karen" and "Larry"?

183 Who is "Sponge Woman"?

184 Who is "The Amazing Awake Lady"?

185 Who are The Sweaty Boys?

186 Who is Mitten Boy?

187 Who is "Agnes From Truthville"?
A. Lisa
B. Fran
C. Jamie

188 Who was "Corporate Sally?"

189 While on vacation as "Burt and Sylvia Buchman," Paul and Jamie pretended to be more people than could comfortably fit in their room! Which of the following personas did they take on?
A. A French girl named Simone
B. A diplomat
C. An acrobat
D. A contortionist
E. The inventor of Cup-a-Soup
F. A rodeo clown
G. A boat hand on the *Calypso*
H. A bomb dismantler
I. A secret service agent
J. A tailor
K. An Italian couple
L. A pro bowler
M. A high-ranking military official
N. An astronaut and his wife
O. Cellists
P. The couple who discovered Velcro
Q. Doctors
R. All of the above

Mad About You Odds and Ends

190 What was the middle name of the "Paul Buchman" who died?

    A. Lloyd

    B. Matthew

    C. David

191 What specific "luxury item" did Paul tell Ira he would buy if he ever hit it really big?

    A. Italian shoes

    B. A $119 pen

    C. A big-screen TV

    D. A really nice hat

192 How old was the inventor of the "virtual reality" device in which Ira wanted Paul to invest?

193 What charity mistakenly took Paul and Jamie's bed?

    A. The Little Sisters of Mercy

    B. Goodwill

    C. The Salvation Army

194 TRUE OR FALSE: The name of the female cabbie who took Paul and Jamie to Yoko Ono's apartment was Rita.

195 The retrieval code for Paul and Jamie's answering machine was a certain number added to Dave Debusschere's jersey number, 22. What was the complete retrieval code?

196 When Jamie attempted spring cleaning, she put clothes into four piles: SAVE, STORAGE, GOODWILL, and _____ ?

    A. UNKNOWN
    B. HIDEOUS
    C. PAISLEY
    D. LISA

197 What exercise device did Paul once buy and wasn't even able to open the box?

    A. The Bullworker
    B. The Belly Buster
    C. Pec-Man!

198 Paul told Jamie that every school had one generically-named guy who was always "friendly." What was this ubiquitous student's name?

199 Before Paul and Jamie borrowed Fran's car to go to the Jersey shore for clams one ridiculously hot summer day, Paul temporarily cooled Jamie off by doing something unusual with her panties. What did he do?

200 What was the name of the unseen racetrack legend whom Paul began pretending he knew?

    A. Tommy
    B. Maurice
    C. Mike

201 What was the name of the fifty to one longshot horse that Jamie and Paul bet on so that they could place Uncle Van's ashes in the winner's circle?

    A. Salisbury Steak
    B. About to Be Glue
    C. Tell Me It's True Baby

202 What kind of camera did future filmmaker Paul Buchman have as a child? (HINT: He took it with him to the third game of the 1964 World Series.)

    A. A Polaroid Land Camera
    B. A Brownie Instamatic
    C. A Nikon

203 TRUE OR FALSE: Paul's video game of choice was Sega.

204 When Paul and Jamie arrived at the Hotel St. Nicole as "Burt and Sylvia Buchman," Paul tipped the bellboy eight beads. How much was that in cash?

    A. 50 cents
    B. $10
    C. $35

Purseona

205 To the delight of Lisa and the frustration of Jamie, the two sisters once accidentally switched purses. From the following list of twenty-one "things," identify in whose purse each item was found.

A. A doll's head
B. Subway tokens
C. Gum
D. A napkin "appointment book"
E. An empty mayonnaise jar
F. An umbrella
G. A *Daily News*
H. An ice bag
I. A baseball glove
J. A wine glass
K. A horseshoe
L. A wine bottle
M. A manicure set
N. A pen
O. A pair of new pantyhose
P. Spray cologne
Q. A clump of raisins
R. A stun gun
S. A puppet
T. An omelet pan
U. Scout, a rabbit

One Last "Also Known As . . ." Question

206 Who was the "Dragon Lady"?

5

Lisa

Anne Ramsay

Lisa is Jamie's sister. And Paul's cross. An irresponsible, irresistible scatterbrain with an eating disorder, Lisa drives Paul and Jamie crazy. How much do you know about the one-of-a-kind Ms. Stemple?

(Scene) *Paul, Jamie, Fran, and Mark are at a party at Lisa's apartment.*

JAMIE   Where's your stove? I thought Mom and
Dad bought you a stove.
LISA   Yeah, I loaned it to a friend.

FRAN   Lisa, you wouldn't happen to have a key that
opens handcuffs would you?
LISA   Over there, top drawer.

LISA (*to Jamie*)   Okay, you always say you know
what I'm feeling. What am I feeling now?
JAMIE   I don't know. I've never felt you feel this
before.
LISA   (*Laughs*) I'm happy!
JAMIE   Oh, my God! You are! How do you like it?
LISA   I don't.

(Scene) *Paul, Jamie, Lisa, and Selby are all on a train to Connecticut for Thanksgiving dinner at the Stemple home.*

LISA   I love Thanksgiving. What a pleasure. I see
Mom and Dad; they awaken my eating disorder
just in time for the holidays. (*Shouts to Selby*)
Where's that pound cake?

207 Which of the following pharmaceuticals is Lisa's antidepressant of choice?

    A. Valium

    B. Lithium

    C. Prozac

    D. Librium

208 TRUE OR FALSE: Paul has seen Jamie's sister Lisa topless.

209 How much older than Jamie is Lisa?

    A. One year

    B. Three years

    C. Five years

    D. They're the same age.

210 TRUE OR FALSE: Lisa graduated high school in three years on an accelerated program.

211 When Lisa's psychiatrist featured her in a book she wrote, what pseudonym did the doctor use for her?

    A. Moira

    B. Edna

    C. Helen

    D. Alicia

212 FILL IN THE BLANK: Lisa was friends with two bulimics named _____ .

213 TRUE OR FALSE: Jamie has a psychic bond with Lisa and can actually keep tabs on her telepathically.

214 Which day of the week did Lisa do her laundry at Paul and Jamie's apartment?

    A. Sunday
    B. Tuesday
    C. Friday
    D. Saturday

215 TRUE OR FALSE: Lisa lives in a ground-floor garden apartment.

216 What actor did Lisa's ex-boyfriend Arthur look like?

    A. Robert Conrad
    B. William Shatner
    C. Tom Cruise
    D. Willem Dafoe

217 TRUE OR FALSE: Lisa graduated from college.

218 Lisa underwent an emotional trauma during what popular Broadway musical (that once featured Marla Maples)?

    A. *Cats*
    B. *The Phantom of the Opera*
    C. *The Will Rogers Follies*
    D. *A Chorus Line*

219 TRUE OR FALSE: Lisa's boyfriend Steven was divorced.

220 TRUE OR FALSE: Lisa has to iron on the top of her toilet because she doesn't have an ironing board.

221 Which of Lisa's friends from group visited her at Paul and Jamie's apartment when Paul and Jamie were away in Vermont?

    A. Harriet

    B. Harriet

    C. Gunther

222 TRUE OR FALSE: Lisa met a guy at Fran's Valentine's Day party when the two of them were shot in the forehead with rubber arrows by Fran's son.

223 Lisa once considered moving in with a British guy named Michael who had had less than good luck with his three previous wives. Match Michael's wife with the way she died:

    A. Delia   1. Was struck by lightning

    B. Amanda   2. Died in a bull run at Pamplona

    C. Fiona   3. Drowned at sea in a flood

224 TRUE OR FALSE: Lisa once worked as Murray's manager.

225 Complete Lisa's two "on spec" fortune cookie fortunes:

    A. "A man who laughs will show his _____ ."

    B. "A whistling _____ man is no _____ man at all."

226 What was the title of the book Lisa's shrink wrote about some of her patients?

    A. *Two Bulimics Named Harriet and Other Case Histories*

    B. *Manics*

    C. *I, Neurotic*

227 Fill in the missing word from the chapter in Lisa's shrink's book that was about Lisa: "Edna on the Road to _____"

228 What sexy actor and star of the movies *Husbands and Wives*, *Leap of Faith*, and *Schindler's List* did Lisa once believe moved into her building?

229 Lisa once dated Troy, a guy who performed a certain personal procedure for her friend Harriet. What did Troy do for a living?
   A. He was an acupuncturist.
   B. He was a hairdresser.
   C. He was a psychic palm reader.

230 What famous Kennedy did Lisa once believe she saw at her health club?
   A. John Kennedy Jr.
   B. Caroline Kennedy
   C. Ethel Kennedy

231 TRUE OR FALSE: Laughing gas made Lisa depressed.

232 Lisa once borrowed a large sum of money from Paul and Jamie, a fact of which Paul felt necessary to periodically remind her. How much did she borrow?
   A. $500
   B. $600
   C. $1,000

233 TRUE OR FALSE: Lisa moved in with Jamie when Paul went to Chicago to shoot a film for two months.

234 When Jamie's mom found out that Jamie had lost her virginity, she bought Lisa an appliance. What was it?

    A. A toaster oven

    B. A microwave

    C. A coffeemaker

235 TRUE OR FALSE: Lisa was living in an illegal sublet.

236 In order to get Lisa to the hospital to have her adenoids removed as a child, her mother told her they were going to a taping of one of Lisa's favorite TV shows. Name the show.

    A. *The Price Is Right*

    B. *The Dating Game*

    C. *The Match Game*

237 Who gave Lisa the couch that Paul and Ira were trying to move the summer day that Murray was towed?

    A. Paul's mother, Sylvia

    B. Jamie

    C. Fran

    D. Paul's father, Burt

238 What did Lisa's boyfriend Dennis do for a living? (HINT: She loved the fact that he visited her everyday and always brought her things.)

239 Lisa felt that Uncle Van's ashes should be scattered in a certain state for a typically ridiculous "Lisa" reason: Because he owned a DeSoto. What state that almost rhymed with DeSoto did Lisa feel would be appropriate as Uncle Van's final resting place?

240 While at the racetrack with Paul, Jamie, and Ira, Lisa bought a certain weather instrument with Secretariat on it. What did she buy?

    A. A thermometer

    B. A barometer

    C. A wind gauge

241 Two people who thought Paul and Jamie were mad at them took Lisa out to lunch in an attempt to find out what they had done wrong. Who were the two who picked up Lisa's (large) lunch tabs?

242 How much did the ferret that Lisa once wanted to buy cost?

    A. $400

    B. $500

    C. $600

243 What did Paul tell Lisa to do when she complained, "I've got fourteen things and three holes. What do I do?"

    A. "Call *Hard Copy*."

    B. "Join the circus."

    C. "Fax Dr. Ruth."

244 Jamie "enhanced" Lisa's resume by saying that she was personal assistant to which very famous reclusive writer?

    A. Thomas Pynchon

    B. J. D. Salinger

    C. Stephen King

245 What was the name of the doll whose head Lisa kept in her purse?

246 TRUE OR FALSE: Lisa's shrink's name was Dr. Wallach.

For Serious Lisa Fans

247 Lisa had a friend named Alice who had a particularly morbid occupation. What did Alice do for a living?
  A. Embalmer
  B. Funeral director
  C. Gravedigger
  D. Morgue worker

248 One of Lisa's former boyfriends was a ventriloquist named Irwin. What was the name of Irwin's dummy?
  A. Charlie
  B. Spats
  C. Splinky
  D. Pooky

"History of Lisa" Questions

249 TRUE OR FALSE: Lisa rented a horse for her prom.

250 What was Lisa wearing on her feet when she broke her toe playing soccer in gym class in December of 1976?
  A. Thongs
  B. Athletic socks
  C. Peds
  D. Nothing. She was barefoot.

251 As a young girl, Lisa used to do something rather bizarre with loose leaf reinforcements. What did she do?

252 TRUE OR FALSE: Lisa once doused her mother's bras in kerosene and ignited them.

253 Which U.S. president did Lisa once believe she had for high school algebra?

    A. Richard Nixon
    B. LBJ
    C. JFK

6

Ira

Ira Buchman is the quintessential New Yorker, as well as being Paul's cousin and best friend. He is also one of the most entertaining characters ever seen in a comedy series. How "Ira-savvy" are you?

(Scene) *Paul and Ira are sitting at a bar after Ira's disastrous fling with Diane "Spy Girl" Caldwell.*

IRA   You know, I once had a thing for Betty Rubble.

PAUL   Animated. She was animated.

IRA   I'd have calmed her down.

PAUL   She was a drawing.

IRA   A man can dream, can't he?

254 TRUE OR FALSE: The first time Ira appears in an episode of *Mad About You* is when Paul and Jamie run into him at a deli.

255 What did Ira do for a living?

    A. First he worked for Paul's father at Buchman's Sporting Goods and then he took over the store.

    B. He was a professional gambler.

    C. He was a professional musician.

    D. He was a butcher.

256 Which of the following exclamations were the first words Ira ever said on *Mad About You?*

    A. "Bite me!"

    B. "What's the matter with you?"

    C. "Hey, hey, hey, look at you two!"

    D. "Bend over!"

257 With which bridesmaid did Ira have a fling at the wedding where he and his band played and which Paul and Jamie (reluctantly) attended?

    A. Cheryl

    B. Lisa

    C. Jennifer

258 TRUE OR FALSE: Paul once lied to Jamie about a trip he took to Atlantic City with Ira during which he lost $400.

259 At Ira's instigation, Paul once pretended to be a certain type of doctor at one of Fran's parties. What was Paul's medical "specialty?"

    A. OB/GYN

    B. Brain surgeon

    C. Chiropractor

    D. Podiatrist

260 TRUE OR FALSE: Ira never mailed Paul's letter to *Spy Girl*.

261 Who scored higher on their SATs, Paul or Ira?

262 To impress girls in bars, with what rock superstar did Ira occasionally pretend to be making a video?

   A. Prince
   B. Bruce Springsteen
   C. Michael Jackson
   D. Paul McCartney

263 Ira had a girlfriend named Mimi who had what unbelievably annoying habit (especially so in theaters!)?

   A. She crunched individual Tic-Tacs for hours at a time.
   B. She mumbled to herself every fifteen seconds.
   C. She hummed constantly.

264 What was Ira's affectionate nickname for his cousin Paulie?

   A. "Pez-Head"
   B. "Splinky"
   C. "Moron"

265 Ira's "ex-wife" (whom he never got around to divorcing) was a brassy blond named Marianne Lugaso. Where did Ira run into her twenty years after they were originally wed?

   A. At a newsstand
   B. In Atlantic City
   C. In Las Vegas
   D. In Minnesota, the "herring capitol of the world"

266 Which of the following show business personalities had their own sandwiches in the Atlantic City casino where Paul and Jamie stayed for the weekend, thanks to Ira?
  A. Victor Borge
  B. Liza Minnelli
  C. Buddy Hackett
  D. Siegfried (of Siegfried and Roy)
  E. All of the above

267 Of what, ahem, "precious metal" was Ira and Marianne's wedding rings made?

268 Paul had a film of Jamie and Fran doing something to each other that Ira found very erotic. What were they doing that so turned Ira on?
  A. Washing each others' hair
  B. Smearing lotion all over each other at Jones Beach
  C. Trying on and modeling swimsuits
  D. Giving each other simultaneous foot massages

269 TRUE OR FALSE: Ira had an illegal cable hookup in his apartment.

270 What popular television detective show did Ira try to convince Paul Steven Spielberg had once directed?
  A. *Columbo*
  B. *Barnaby Jones*
  C. *Matlock*

271 What gift of footware did Ira give Jamie for her thirtieth birthday?

    A. Slippers

    B. Running shoes

    C. High heels

272 What was Ira wearing on his head the summer day he and Paul tried to move a couch for Lisa?

    A. A turban

    B. A toupée

    C. A baseball cap

    D. A fez

273 Which of the following twelve-step programs did Ira attend?

    A. Alcoholics Anonymous

    B. Overeaters Anonymous

    C. Gamblers Anonymous

274 What song was Ira's band supposed to play in the Thanksgiving Day parade before they got bumped?

    A. "Turkey in the Straw"

    B. "The Alley Cat"

    C. "New York, New York"

275 What act bumped Ira's band from the Thanksgiving Day parade?

    A. Barney

    B. Shari Lewis and Lambchop

    C. Underdog

276 TRUE OR FALSE: Ira has a key to Paul and Jamie's apartment.

277 Once, when Paul and Jamie's toilet was out of commission, Ira had to pee. Where did he end up relieving himself? (HINT: After learning what Ira used, Paul told Jamie they would now have to move.)
  A. In the bathroom sink
  B. In the bathtub
  C. In the kitchen sink

278 What was Paul's nickname for his cousin Ira?
  A. "Splinky"
  B. "Pez-Head"
  C. "Mookie"

279 Ira once dated a girl named Velma who Paul and Jamie thought was a world class liar. From the following list of claims, identify the ones Velma made, which Paul and Jamie didn't believe:
  A. Velma said she was a member of the original Go-Gos.
  B. Velma said that in the "Vacation" video, she was the one skiing slalom.
  C. Velma said she managed Aerosmith.
  D. Velma said she attended NYU Film School.
  E. Velma said she knew Liza Minnelli.
  F. Velma said she was once an impostor for Caroline Kennedy on *To Tell the Truth*.

G. Velma said she finished the New York City Marathon in the top ten.

H. Velma said she was J. D. Salinger's niece and had read some of his unpublished stories.

280 Ira prevented Jamie's friend Susannah from pocketing a pack of matches Paul and Jamie had brought home from vacation. What Las Vegas act matches did Susannah want to take?

A. Siegfried and Roy

B. Buddy Hackett

C. Cirque De Soleil

281 Who was Ira's roommate in the year prior to Paul and Jamie moving in together?

A. Cosmo Kramer

B. Paul

C. Marianne Lugaso

A "Family History" True or False Question

282 Paul and Ira bathed together every night when they were kids.

For Serious Ira Fans

283 How tall is Ira?

A. Five feet five

B. Five feet nine-and-a-half

C. Six feet

(PHOTOFEST)

7

Murray

Proud papa Murray with a member of his new family.

There's a *Mad About You* rumor hinting that Murray the
dog gets almost as much fan mail as Paul Reiser and
Helen Hunt. That's only right, don't you think?

284 Where did Paul find Murray?

    A. In the subway

    B. In Connecticut

    C. At the Bronx Zoo

    D. In Central Park

285 TRUE OR FALSE: Murray is a purebred collie.

286 TRUE OR FALSE: Murray's across-the-hall paramour
Sophie was a Cairn terrier show dog.

287 During his and Jamie's first meeting, Paul facetiously
asked the newsstand guy for a magazine for Murray. What
was the name of this mag?

    A. *Dog's Life*

    B. *Bow WOW!*

    C. *The Paws*

    D. *Curb and Hydrant*

288 Which of the following commands did Murray know
how to obey?

    A. Sit

    B. Beg

    C. Speak

    D. None of the above

289 TRUE OR FALSE: Ira was with Paul the night he found Murray.

290 TRUE OR FALSE: Jamie has a Murrayness.

291 Lisa once accidentally switched Murray with the Beckners' dog Simon. What did Janey Beckner do for a living?
>   A. She was a neurosurgeon.
>   B. She was in PR.
>   C. She was unemployed.

292 What word did the Beckners use that Paul and Jamie had to go look up?
>   A. "invectify"
>   B. "dysphoric"
>   C. "puerile"
>   D. "pedagogue"

293 After Murray's "rendezvous" with the Conway's dog Sophie, Paul realized that Murray liked terriers. Paul had always thought Murray preferred another type of dog, specifically a breed known for very fancy haircuts. Name this breed.

294 What was Murray doing that prompted Paul to say, "See? If I could do that, why would I be going out tonight?"

295 Paul once described Murray as "a _____ with organs."

296 What is "The Murray Box"?

297 What was Murray's name before Paul found him?
  A. Swifty
  B. Maui
  C. Eddie

298 What was Murray's mother's name?
  A. Grace
  B. Janice
  C. Mona

299 What specifically was Murray doing one day that prompted Paul to remark, "This is new"?

300 How many puppies did Sophie and Murray have?

301 Murray not only ate Paul and Jamie's Thanksgiving turkey, he also got into one other course from that day's meal. What was it?
  A. The candied yams
  B. The salad
  C. The dessert

302 What rock band once used Murray in one of their videos?
  A. Aerosmith
  B. Megadeth
  C. Counting Crows

303 What was the name of the one-hour television drama that Murray auditioned for and deliberately messed up so as not to cause problems between Paul and Jamie?

    A. *Relative Matters*

    B. *Parents*

    C. *My New Family*

304 How old was Murray when he became "an actor?"

For Seriously *Mad* Fans

305 When Lisa lost Murray, Paul and Jamie went to the police station where Sergeant Panino helped them fill out the report. What was the name of Panino's dog?

    A. Pete

    B. Swifty

    C. Maui

Fran and Mark Devanow

Richard Kind (Mark Devanow) mingling at a 1994 television
convention.

This chapter tests your knowledge of the Devanows, two of Paul and Jamie's closest—and most "interesting"— friends.

Fran

306 TRUE OR FALSE: Paul once saw Fran naked.

307 TRUE OR FALSE: When it came to sex, Fran liked being on the bottom.

308 The day Paul ran into Mark in a New York City restaurant, Fran was having a "good _____ day." What body part was Fran especially proud of that day?

    A. "ass"
    B. "boob"
    C. "hair"
    D. "thigh"

309 Fran told Jamie that she had had sex with Sergio the doorman and that she might be pregnant. With whom did Fran *really* sleep (and was embarrassed to tell Jamie about)?

310 What animated character did Fran's son say he wanted as his mother in a fit of childish petulance?

    A. Betty Rubble
    B. The Little Mermaid
    C. Beauty
    D. Snow White

311 TRUE OR FALSE: Fran hated exercising and never jogged.

312 What was Fran's nickname for Mark?
- A. Pooky
- B. Splinky
- C. Kooky
- D. Snooky

313 To dress up the apartment for Paul's fifteen-minute documentary, Fran lent Jamie a painting by a Dadaist that had been on display at MoMA. Can you name this painter?
- A. Mowa
- B. Ernst
- C. Duchamp
- D. Man Ray

314 On what classic kid's television show did Fran appear as a child?
- A. *Wonderama*
- B. *The Mickey Mouse Club*
- C. *Romper Room*

315 Fran once wrote a commercial for a client that used Don Mattingly on a horse in Yankee Stadium. The client insisted that Fran replace Mattingly with what fiery singer?
- A. Bette Midler
- B. Chita Rivera
- C. Shirley MacLaine

For Serious Fran Fans

316 FILL IN THE BLANK: As a child, Fran was _____ champion at Camp Wokahona for three years running.

317 Fran was born on October 28. Name the year.
- A. 1960
- B. 1963
- C. 1965

Mark

318 TRUE OR FALSE: Mark proposed to Fran on top of the Empire State Building.

319 What was Paul talking about when he told Mark, "Bite it off! Be a man!"

320 After Fran and Mark split up, what hotel did Mark move into?
- A. The Chelsea Plaza
- B. The Regency
- C. The Hilton

321 Which of the following activities did Mark tell Paul he wanted to try after splitting up with Fran?
- A. Shoot the rapids
- B. Go to Carnivale in Rio
- C. Dance on the Great Wall of China
- D. All of the above

322 What is Mark's middle name?

323 TRUE OR FALSE: Mark believed that burial at sea was a "very soothing" idea.

324 What was Mark's job when Paul discovered him working in a diner in New York City?
   A. He was a short-order cook.
   B. He owned the restaurant.
   C. He was a busboy.

325 TRUE OR FALSE: Mark's sister lived in New Rochelle.

326 How did Mark repeatedly mispronounce the title of the movie *Easy Rider*?
   A. He kept calling it *THE Easy Rider*.
   B. He kept calling it *Easy Glider*.
   C. He kept calling it *The Rider*.

327 YES OR NO? Did Mark find Omar Sharif attractive?

328 Who is "Antonio" and what does this have to do with Mark?

329 Which of the following magazines did Mark read while living in a hotel after he moved out on Fran?
   A. *Surfer Digest*
   B. *Log Cabin Monthly*
   C. *Soldier of Fortune*
   D. All of the above

330 TRUE OR FALSE: Mark once had a dream about Pierce Brosnan.

For Serious Mark Fans

331 Match the geographic location with Mark's activities while he was in each of these places:

A. Wisconsin	1. Auditioned for clown school
B. West Virginia	2. Manufactured beef jerky
C. Abilene	3. Lived on the beach with two girls
D. Tallahassee	4. Worked as a merchant marine
E. Albuquerque	5. Dated a twenty-three-year-old
F. Hawaii	6. Worked as a coal miner
G. Tupelo	7. Ate only okra

332 What poem did Fran and Mark's son plan on reciting for his grandmother during their Thanksgiving visit?
- A. "Hiawatha"
- B. "Casey at the Bat"
- C. "The Raven"
- D. "The Cat in the Hat"

333 YES OR NO? Did Mark and Fran have a security system in their apartment?

334 What was Paul's "affectionate" nickname for Mark and Fran's son, Ryan?
- A. "Devil child"
- B. "Satan's spawn"
- C. "The Buchmans' curse"

335 What did Paul tell Mark and Fran's son to make him stop singing "Do You Know the Muffin Man?" on the phone?

336 In the spurious Thanksgiving story Paul told Fran and Mark's son on the train, what was the name of the head Pilgrim?
  A. Phil
  B. Ed
  C. Norman
  D. Chuck

337 What did Fran and Mark's accountant have in common with Jamie and Paul's dog?

338 TRUE OR FALSE: Fran and Mark had an illegal cable hookup in their apartment.

The "Not So Much" Happy Couple

339 The year Mark left Fran, how much money did he make as a OB/GYN?
  A. $100,000
  B. $300,000
  C. $500,000

For Sharp-Eyed *Mad About You* Fans

340 What was Fran and Mark's apartment number?

9

Parents
and Relatives

Helen Hunt as seen in one of her early films, the 1987 sci fi thriller *Project X*.

Parents. Relatives. Need I say more?

(Scene) *Paul and Jamie are debating whether or not to put out an atrocious ceramic fish that Jamie's mother gave them.*

JAMIE   If she doesn't see it, she's gonna start smiling.
PAUL   Well, we don't want *that* to happen.
JAMIE   No, no, no, trust me. If she smiles, she's hurt. If she laughs, she's pissed. She gets bubbly, it's every man for himself.

(Scene) *Fran has arrived at the Buchmans' relatives-filled apartment while Paul and Jamie were out buying overlooked Thanksgiving dinner "necessities."*

FRAN   I've been here *minutes!*
PAUL   Listen, I've been with them years. Trust me, it gets worse.

The Stemples

341 What was Gus and Theresa Stemples' nickname for their daughter Jamie?

   A. Pumpkin
   B. Peanut
   C. Shortcake
   D. Bubbles

342 TRUE OR FALSE: Jamie's father liked Gulden's mustard.

343 Uncle Van once implanted a certain type of "sporting good" in Jamie's mother's Thanksgiving turkey. What was it?
  A. A selection of golf tees
  B. A jock strap
  C. An assortment of golf balls

344 TRUE OR FALSE: Uncle Van's wake took place at the Everly Chapel Funeral Home.

345 Who took Uncle Van's ashes home?
  A. Jamie
  B. Lisa
  C. Ira

346 TRUE OR FALSE: Jamie's mom used to be an actress when she was young.

347 When Paul and Jamie's had everyone at their place for Thanksgiving, Jamie's dad Gus issued three "It's a fact!" proclamations. Which of the following was not one of Gus's "facts!"?
  A. Shari Lewis is Jerry Lewis's wife.
  B. "Vegetarians die young!"
  C. $179 minimum for a plumber on Thanksgiving.
  D. Regis Philbin is Mike Douglas's son.

The Buchmans

348 At what musical did Paul's father Burt say hello to Regis Philbin?

    A. *Cats*

    B. *Grease*

    C. *Moby!*

349 Which of Paul's uncles prepared his and Jamie's wills?

350 How long was Sylvia in labor with Paul?

351 TRUE OR FALSE: Paul's mother once bought Paul and Jamie an electric blanket, even though Jamie hated electric blankets.

352 What was the name of Paul's Uncle Jules's wife?

    A. Bev

    B. Sylvia

    C. Ethel

    D. Lucy

353 After collapsing at work, Paul's father had to be rushed to Beth Israel Medical Center. What caused him to collapse?

    A. He "overdid the Stairmaster."

    B. He fell asleep under a sun lamp.

    C. He tried to move a pool table by himself.

    D. He was demonstrating a fly fishing rod and threw his back out.

354 What did Paul's mother give Jamie for her thirtieth birthday?

  A. An answering machine

  B. A vacuum cleaner

  C. A purse

355 What was Paul's mother Sylvia's favorite "girl" name (as she loved to repeatedly remind Paul and Jamie)?

  A. Barbara

  B. Sylvia

  C. Annabelle

356 What year did Sylvia and Burt Buchman move into their apartment?

  A. 1945

  B. 1954

  C. 1965

357 TRUE OR FALSE: Burt Buchman's "Buchman's Sporting Goods" commercial director for twenty years was named Morty.

358 What musical instrument did Paul's father make him take as a kid?

  A. Flute

  B. Clarinet

  C. Guitar

Miscellaneous Kin

359 Which of the Buchmans' relatives once dated Alan Brady?

A. Paul's mother, Sylvia
B. Aunt Lolly
C. Jamie's mother, Theresa

360 When she was young, Aunt Lolly used to play a certain musical instrument in Grossinger's lobby. Name this instrument.

A. Harp
B. Accordion
C. Piano

361 TRUE OR FALSE: Paul always called Jamie's cousin Jeanette "Arlene."

362 During a conversation about Harvey Keitel, which of Paul and Jamie's relatives once said, "I don't care for his penis"? (Which caused Helen Hunt/Jamie Buchman to do a truly excellent spit take.)

A. Paul's mother, Sylvia
B. Jamie's mother, Theresa
C. Lisa

For Seriously *Mad* Fans

363 Paul's mother's friend Sylvia's brother Herb had a very strange job. What was it?

A. He stamped the "M & M" on M & Ms.
B. He sold mattresses door-to-door.
C. He put the worm into bottles of tequila.
D. He was a pet psychiatrist.

10

Ursula

Lisa Kudrow

Ah, Ursula. Ditz personified. Waitress extraordinaire. If you happen to live on Saturn, that is. Ursula works at Riff's and usually waits (well, she tries) on Paul and Jamie when they eat there. You can order anything from Ursula. That doesn't mean you'll get it, but at least you can say you tried.

(Scene) *Paul and Jamie are sitting at a table at Riff's.*

URSULA   Here you go!

PAUL   This is what?

URSULA   That's your check. Unless you want to get something else.

PAUL   I thought we'd order dinner first.

URSULA   Oh, right. So what can I get you?

PAUL   Menus?

364 TRUE OR FALSE: Ursula hated her name.

365 In addition to waitressing at Riff's, Ursula also worked another job. What was it?

A. Masseuse

B. Tour guide at the Museum of Natural History

C. Stand-up comedian

D. Clerk at a health food store

366 TRUE OR FALSE: Ursula once delivered menus to Paul and Jamie in their bedroom.

367 Ursula once refilled Paul's tea cup with something that was not tea. Name it.

    A. Decaf coffee

    B. Ice water

    C. Sangria

368 How many of Paul and Jamie's credit cards did Ursula cut up when told to by the "man on the phone"?

369 YES OR NO? Did Ursula and Ira ever date?

370 TRUE OR FALSE: Ursula remembered lending her mittens to Jamie.

371 What man's name did Ursula once call Lisa?

    A. Gary

    B. Ira

    C. Raoul

    D. Paul

372 What was the name of Ursula's twin sister?

Crossover Dreams

373 Where did Ursula's twin work?

(PHOTOFEST)

11

Selby

Tommy Hinkley

Selby was only seen in the first season. Do *you* remember him?

> (Scene) *On the train ride to Connecticut for Thanksgiving dinner at the Stemple home, Paul and Selby are chatting while waiting to get into the bathroom.*

SELBY   I'm seriously considering donating my
sperm to an anonymous lesbian couple.
PAUL   That'll be nice: Turning your hobby into
something useful.
SELBY   Exactly!

❤ ❤

374 TRUE OR FALSE: Selby and Paul went to college together.

375 How much did Lisa pay Selby to pretend he was her boyfriend during her Thanksgiving visit home?

A. $10
B. $25
C. $50
D. $100

376 TRUE OR FALSE: Selby once finished a 10K race by cheating.

377 YES OR NO? One of Selby's dates was a girl named Dora. Did Dora have a sister?

378 At what restaurant did Selby run into Paul's old girlfriend, Lynne Stoddard?

    A. The Papaya King
    B. The Russian Tea Room
    C. McDonald's
    D. Riff's

379 What was the last line ever spoken by Selby on the show?

    A. "I'm outta here."
    B. "You are such a goofus."
    C. "Masha, thank you."

380 TRUE OR FALSE: Selby was Selby's first name.

(PHOTOFEST)

Madly Quotable

This chapter quizzes you on some of the best—and funniest—remarks and comments ever uttered in a network sitcom. Be forewarned, though: These questions might be a little tough. (But they're still fun!)

381 What was Jamie's provocative response when Paul remarked, "If I had two tongues I'd be the happiest person in the world," as he was licking wedding invitation envelopes in the one-hour "wedding" episode?

382 After Paul insulted an NBC executive at one of Fran's parties, Lisa came up to him and said, "Scrod?" What did Paul reply?

383 Paul's motto was "Be prepared." Whose motto was "Never marry anyone more neurotic than yourself"?

384 Who was Paul talking about when he told Jamie, "They'll be dead in five years"?

385 What did Paul reply to Jamie's question, "How come my parents can still push all my buttons?"

386 Who said, "I have so much pain inside me that I can cry at will"?
   A. Lisa
   B. Fran
   C. Lou
   D. Ira

387 Why in the world did Jamie once actually say to Paul, "Go show Fran your penis"? (HINT: "stirrups")

388 About whom was Fran talking when she told Paul, "Don't thwart him. He doesn't like to be thwarted."

389 Who said, "Neighbors are nothing but trouble"?
- A. Paul
- B. Jamie
- C. Ira
- D. Fran

390 Who said, "I'm uneasy with starting a cheese"?

391 TRUE OR FALSE: According to Jamie, Woody Allen once said "Wow!" about Paul's work.

392 Who said, "I'm a handsome, handsome man," while looking in the mirror?

393 How did Paul's cameraman Warren respond when Connie asked him, "Did you ever see a dachshund with nerve damage?"
- A. "Once, in Berlin."
- B. "No, but my budgie had a migraine the other day."
- C. "Yes, but she was with someone."
- D. "Why, are you missing one?"

394 About whom was Masha the maid talking when she said, "You are soft like woman"?

    A. Ira

    B. Paul

    C. Mark

    D. Selby

395 To whom was Fran speaking when she said, "You toyed with the affections of an immigrant"?

396 According to Paul, what do guys say when girls give in on the first date?

397 What environmental topic was Paul talking about when he exclaimed, "I'm really losing patience with the Earth!"?

A *Mad About You* "Classic Moments" Question

398 "Who's Annette!?"

399 To whom was Ira talking when he said, "Your head has good bounce"?

400 Who once asked Paul the question, "If you're married a million years, does your wedding album go platinum?"

401 To what "couple" was Jamie referring when she described their first "date" as, "like a David Lynch version of *When Harry Met Sally . . .*"?

402 What was Mark describing when he said, "It's like pulling three pot roasts out of a Pringles can"?

403 Who once said, "My schmeckie's in the *Post*!"?

404 When playing Little League as a kid, how did Paul feel about running from first to second base?

    A. He loved second base because he didn't have to share it with anyone else.

    B. He thought it superfluous.

    C. He said, "I'm uncomfortable with second base."

405 Who told Jamie, "Guys always want the boom. We just made up the bing and the bang to get to the boom"?

    A. Paul

    B. Ira

    C. Warren

    D. Mark

406 To whom was Sylvia Buchman speaking when she said, "My God, can't you skip a night!?"

407 Who said, "We're a lot more self-absorbed than most people."

408 About whom was Jamie talking when she said, "They're not even funny!"

409 Who asked Jamie, "I have no job, no prospects, no interests, no hobbies, bad hair, I'm PMSing . . . do you think he'll like me?", Lisa or Fran?

410 Who said, "How come every time I meet a great girl she's in love with my cousin?"

411 About whom is Paul talking about here: "[He's] a phone-toting, plaid-pant-wearing, film-cutting, back-stabbing, son-of-a-bitch!'"?

412 Who once told Paul, "My windows were stolen"?

413 Who was Jamie addressing when she said, "You're a little, little man"?

414 What did Paul once describe as "soft and good"?

415 Match the Chinese Bowl fortune cookie with the recipient:

    A. "Sunny smiles make for pleasant days."   1. Fran

    B. "Bad luck follows the guilty."   2. Paul

    C. "You are loved by many."   3. Ira

    D. "Your wife is guilty and you're right all the time."   4. Jamie

Fill in the Blank of Paul's "Made-Up" Fortune

416 "When in doubt, cut to the _____."

417 What was Paul talking about when he asked himself, "What's that . . . soup?"

418 What did Jamie respond to Paul's question, "Can the lemon in a lemon muffin go bad?" (HINT: That ain't no lemon.)

419 Complete Paul's rather unique spin on family life: "The grass on other people's _____ is always greener."

420 About whom was Hal Conway talking when he said, "It's like living with a brook"?

421 To whom was Paul talking when he said, "Tea and The Beatles. Ever since then it's nothing but trouble with you people!"?

Give me a five dollar wheel on the six horse, front and back, and give me a 6-3-1 box. Give me a thirty dollar baseball, 1-3-6. Also on the six, let me have ten dollars across the board. *Slap me!* Give me twenty to win, twenty to place, and twenty to show.

—Jamie's winning racetrack bet

---

422 Which of Jamie's relatives was best known for his racetrack exhortation, "Tell me it's true, baby, tell me it's true!"?

    A. Her father Gus
    B. Her Aunt Lolly
    C. Uncle Van

423 What did Sloopy Dunbar say the first time he saw Fran?

    A. "Cut off my legs and call me Shorty!"
    B. "Pierce my ears and call me Ruth!"
    C. "Call my mama, I'm feeling faint!"

424 What did Paul yell to Lisa on the phone when he spoke to her with his foot as he was putting up camera equipment for his fifteen-minute documentary?

    A. "I'm looking at roots!"

    B. "Janet Leigh's co-ops!"

    C. "Chicken à la King!"

425 FILL IN THE BLANK: When Paul and Jamie accidentally interrupted a neighbor couple having sex, he said, "It's like talking to a _____ here."

426 What was Paul talking about when he said, "It seemed like a Gandhi-esque thing to do"?

427 What was Paul talking about when he told Jamie, "It's naked and fun and I agree with both of them"?

428 When Paul asked Aunt Lolly if she had ever gone out with Milton Berle, she admitted, "It's true!" To what legendary showbiz rumor about Berle was Lolly referring with this exclamation?

429 Who once said, "I have PMS and a stun gun. Who's gonna bother me?"

    A. Lisa

    B. Fran

    C. Jamie

430 What was the "correct" response Paul wanted when he asked Jamie if he was losing all his hair?

    A. "Yeah."

    B. "Just a little."

    C. "No, not at all."

13

Work

◀

Paul, Jamie, and the Justice of the Peace/utility worker
who married them, Lyle Lovett.

Paul and Jamie both have had career troubles throughout their married years, and yet even with Paul frequently between projects and Jamie quitting her job, they were still able to pay the rent on what has to be one of the most spacious apartments in New York City. I guess Paul's share in the sporting goods store sure pays off, eh?

Paul's Films

431 What is the name of Paul's production company?

A. Sprockets & Celluloid, Inc.

B. Buchman Films

C. PB and Jamie Productions

D. Murrayland Films

432 To what cable television network did Paul think he accidentally sent his and Jamie's amateur porno tape?

A. ESPN

B. CNN

C. The Family Network

D. MTV

433 What is the name of Paul's agent?

A. David

B. Stephen

C. Paul

D. Janet

434 TRUE OR FALSE: Paul's editor Sid never worked on Alan Brady's variety show.

What's Your *Mad About You* I.Q?

435 What was the title of Paul's documentary about animal behavior? (HINT: It was not a title he was thrilled with.)

    A. *A Day at the Zoo*

    B. *Animal Antics*

    C. *Zoo*

    D. *Beastly Behavior*

436 What homespun television show with a whistled theme song did Paul watch while researching his "History of TV" documentary?

437 Paul's documentary about the first Iraqi-born janitor to work at the Pentagon lost Paul a coveted award to a film having to do with the sea. What was it?

    A. *The Trouble With Barnacles*

    B. *Hello, Coral!*

    C. *Calling All Clams!*

438 What was the title of Paul's documentary about the guy who did amazing scientific tricks with common household items?

    A. *Science Anyone?*

    B. *Mr. Science*

    C. *The Wonderful World of Science*

439 What prestigious film award did Paul *really* want to win?

    A. A Klieg Award

    B. A Silver Sprocket Award

    C. The Annual View/Finder Achievement Award

    D. A Focus Award

118

440 What was the title of Paul's "baseball" documentary?

    A. *The Greatest of Games*

    B. *The House That Ruth Built*

    C. *Strike Zone*

    D. *BatMen*

441 What was the name of the advertising campaign for which Jamie hired Paul to direct a commercial?

    A. The "New York, New York, a Helluva Town!" campaign

    B. The "Come Home to the Equator" Central America campaign

    C. The "I Still Love New York" campaign

    D. The "Yum Yum Yum Yum" Bubblegum campaign

442 In Paul's New York commercial, the guy who played the Big Apple went to Juilliard with what famous comedian/actor?

    A. Jerry Seinfeld

    B. Robin Williams

    C. Tim Allen

    D. Paul Reiser

443 Which of the following segments did Alan Brady insist Paul put back into his documentary about the history of television?

    A. The bowling sketch

    B. The piano player with an itch sketch

    C. Singing with Fabian

    D. All of the above

444 What was the title of Paul's documentary about New York at night?

445 What was the name of the production company that commissioned Paul's "New York at Night" documentary?
   A. City Films
   B. Moving Pictures
   C. CineGroup

446 Pierre, Lola, Colin, Vernon, and Mr. Ching all have something in common having to do with Paul's work. What is it?

447 Of the following projects, which one did Paul end up getting?
   A. The Harvey Keitel thing
   B. The soap opera
   C. The seatbelt instructional video

448 FILL IN THE BLANK: While brainstorming title ideas for his new project, Paul came up with the following. Fill in the missing word. (HINT: For each title, it's the *same* word.)
   A. "The Good, the Bad, and the _____ "
   B. "Robin Hood, Prince of _____ "
   C. "_____ Gump"
   D. "_____ in Seattle"

449 How many filmmakers (including Paul) participated in the "fifteen-minute documentary" project?

450 What cable network hired Paul to do a documentary about the history of television?

    A. HBO

    B. Showtime

    C. Bravo

    D. Nickelodeon

451 While "dressing the set" (which was really nothing but straightening up the apartment) for his fifteen-minute documentary, Paul threw a pair of red socks on the bed and said it was to add a splash of color, like the little girl in a certain Academy Award-winning movie. Name this flick.

    A. *Rain Man*

    B. *Schindler's List*

    C. *Driving Miss Daisy*

    D. *The Silence of the Lambs*

452 What is the title of the salacious B-movie Paul once directed under a pseudonym?

    A. *Bikini Paradise*

    B. *Hooter Carwash II*

    C. *Hooter Vacation*

    D. *Bitch With a Gun*

453 Which of Paul's documentaries had to be edited so that the word "oodles" was replaced with "a tremendous amount"?

    A. His baseball film

    B. *A Day in the Life of a Button*

    C. His Japanese garden documentary

454 What was the title of Paul's documentary about stuccoing roofs?

  A. *You, Too, Can Stucco*
  B. *How to Stucco Your Roof*
  C. *Stucco for One and All*

455 What was the title of Paul's documentary about how to successfully meet someone and "make them yours"?

  A. *How to Find Them, Meet Them, and Make Them Yours*
  B. *Looking for Love in All the Right Places*
  C. *Ten Easy Steps to Making Them Mad About You*

456 What was the name of the gum commercial Murray appeared in?

  A. Gummy Gummy Gum
  B. Yum Yum Gum
  C. Yummy Gummy

457 Which of the following film luminaries did Paul's editor Ike claim to have known?

  A. Martin Scorsese
  B. Alfred Hitchcock
  C. Orson Welles
  D. All of the above

458 What famous TV star did Paul want to host his documentary about television?

  A. Sid Caesar
  B. Alan Brady
  C. Milton Berle

459 According to Paul's assistant Stacey, what did the initials "PBS" stand for?

A. Pretty Bad Stuff
B. Petty Boring Snots
C. Pretentious Boring Snobs
D. Plenty of British Slop

460 Who signed the 1956 World Series Yankees program Jamie gave to Paul to console him when PBS passed on his baseball documentary?

A. George Steinbrenner
B. Ethel Merman
C. Carl Reiner
D. Sloopy Dunbar

461 What cable network hired Paul to shoot a documentary about a Yukon dog sled race?

A. ESPN
B. ESPN2
C. HBO

462 TRUE OR FALSE: One of the items Paul's assistant Connie asked on job applications was "Favorite soup?"

463 What was Paul's cameraman Warren's real first name?

A. Lloyd
B. Sid
C. Eddie

464 TRUE OR FALSE: Before he became Paul's new "producer," Lou Bonaparte was in accounting.

465 Who replaced Connie as Paul's assistant?

    A. Jamie

    B. Fran

    C. Remy

466 Paul's producer Lou was very proud of having directed a musical production in Montclair. What did Lou direct? (HINT: Think "Jerry Lewis")

    A. *Brigadoon*

    B. *Damn Yankees*

    C. *The Music Man*

467 TRUE OR FALSE: In order to prevent Lou from "hovering" over his shoulder, Paul made him sit behind a line in the editing room.

Jamie's Jobs

468 Fill in the missing name from the public relations firm for which Jamie went to work after graduating college: Farrer and _____

469 How long did it take for Jamie to be promoted at the public relations firm where she worked with Fran?

    A. Five years

    B. Five months

    C. Three years

    D. One year

470 Which of the following was NOT one of Jamie's advertising accounts?

    A. Computron

    B. New York Tourism

    C. Central America Tourism

    D. Poultry Producers of America

471 Paul once mistakenly described Jamie's PR title as "Regional Account Manager." What was her *actual* job title?

    A. Regional Vice President

    B. District Manager

    C. Account Supervisor

    D. Territory Manager

472 What was the name of Jamie's male assistant before she quit her PR job?

    A. Rick

    B. Nick

    C. Warren

    D. Ira

473 TRUE OR FALSE: When Paul first tracked Jamie down to where she worked, the receptionist on Fran's floor was a woman named Cheryl.

474 TRUE OR FALSE: When Jamie quit her job, she took a six-pack of Cremora and a fax machine from the office on leaving.

475 On New Year's Day in 1950, Jamie's boss, Manny, played first trombone during a Bowl game halftime. In which Bowl game did he play?

    A. The Rose Bowl

    B. The Super Bowl

    C. The Citrus Bowl

    D. The Orange Bowl

476 During Paul's first meeting with the Director of Tourism for New York, which of the following words did he suggest to Jamie as "emergency codewords"?

    A. "logarithm"

    B. "spittoon"

    C. "Estes Kefauver"

    D. "paramecium"

    E. All of the above

477 TRUE OR FALSE: Jamie's male assistant's duties included checking her teeth for visible food and her pantyhose for snags or runs.

478 Complete Jamie's off-the-cuff tourism slogan: "Central America: Come _____ to the Equator!"

479 After the Central American tourism meeting, what was the insulting remark Jamie's boss made that caused her to quit?

    A. "Latin men love blondes!"

    B. "Aren't you glad you have me around to pick you up when you fall?"

    C. "So you won one? Big deal. You'll still never make partner."

480 Who took Jamie's PR job after she quit?

481 What was the promotional gimmick Jamie came up with for Buchman's Sporting Goods after Ira took over the store?

    A. The character "Crazy Ira"

    B. Buchman Bucks

    C. Crazy Sundays: 20 Percent Off Every Sunday

Personnel File

482 Howie Balenger's supervisor ended up with a producer credit on Howie's breakthrough film. What was this guy's name?

    A. Raoul

    B. Jules

    C. Lloyd

    D. Sirajul

483 What was the title of Howie Balenger's breakthrough film?

    A. *Tunnel of Love*

    B. *The Token Clerk*

    C. *Tunnel of Hate*

    D. *Hating Paul*

484 By whom was Masha the maid employed when she came to work at Paul and Jamie's apartment?

    A. Lisa

    B. Fran and Mark

    C. Ira

    D. Warren

485 YES OR NO? Was Masha from Leningrad?

486 What big science fiction movie did Paul's former assistant, Ricky Gold, direct (much to Paul's dismay)?
   A. *Matrix*
   B. *The Tachyon Tunnel*
   C. *Perpetron*

487 For what baseball team did Sloopy Dunbar play?
   A. The Red Sox
   B. The Yankees
   C. The Twins

488 On which famous dog star did Murray's agent Bob pass?
   A. Lassie
   B. Rin-Tin-Tin
   C. Beethoven

One Final Career Question

489 What was the title of Paul's legendary (to him and Jamie anyway) documentary about a certain garment district item?
   A. *Suede: A History*
   B. *The Collar Wars of 1970*
   C. *A Day in the Life of a Button*
   D. *The Cuff Issue*

14

Clothing
and Jewelry

Paul Reiser as seen in his 1990 film *Crazy People*.

Paul and Jamie had *two* dry cleaners. No wonder this book has a separate "Clothing" chapter!

> (Scene) *Paul, Jamie, Fran, and Ira are at a Chinese restaurant discussing the extra blouse (later christened the "Blouse of Death") that was unintentionally put into Jamie's bag during a shopping trip.*

FRAN Well, I think you should keep the beige one and give them back the taupe.

IRA What is taupe?

PAUL Taupe. It's like beige.

JAMIE No it's not. The two I bought are beige.

FRAN I though the first one was tan.

JAMIE It looked tan but it was beige.

IRA So that sweater I bought was beige?

JAMIE That was off-white.

FRAN More like a camel.

IRA That guy never said camel.

PAUL 'Course not. Camel's not a selling point.

IRA Does that sweater make me look lumpy?

JAMIE No.

FRAN I'm getting a headache.

Underwear

490 On the front of Ira's souvenir "Burt Shirt" T-shirt was a picture of Burt Buchman. What was on the back?

491 What kind of clothing did Paul believe was for "men who live in Crete"?

Clothes R Us

492 Who did Jamie feel dressed like a "manic depressive Psych professor"?

493 What color was the big parka Paul bought to wear for the two months he shot a film in Chicago?
   A. Red
   B. Orange
   C. Yellow

494 TRUE OR FALSE: Paul's father once bought Jamie a feathered jacket that "molted."

495 What color was the Blouse of Death?
   A. Beige
   B. Tan
   C. Off-white
   D. Taupe

496 Jamie's dad Gus once gave Paul a tie with aquatic animals on it. What were they?
   A. Seals
   B. Ducks
   C. Dolphins

497 Uncle Van was a big fan of a certain type of rather loud fashion "style." What was it?

498 Jamie told Paul to wear his parka to shoot his outdoor gum commercial or else he'd freeze. He froze. What did Paul wear instead?

    A. A nylon windbreaker

    B. A wool sportcoat

    C. His suede jacket

Jewelry and Gifts

499 From whom did Paul buy Jamie's engagement ring (with a little help from Fran)?

500 Paul's mom Sylvia once gave Jamie a piece of jewelry that Jamie complained hurt her back. What was it?

    A. A very long neckchain

    B. A very heavy brooch

    C. A big silver bangle bracelet

501 Which of the following potential Valentine's Day gifts would Jamie have preferred to Paul's *actual* gift of skates?

    A. Flowers

    B. A hibachi

    C. Candy

    D. Earrings

    E. A computer

    F. A brooch

    G. A bracelet

    H. A book

    I. A peignoir

Food

Food plays a very important role in Paul and Jamie's lives. They seem to be always snacking, or cooking, or ordering takeout, or just *talking* about food. How much do you remember about these *Mad* morsels?

A *Mad About You* Menu

502 TRUE OR FALSE: Jamie hates chocolates because they give her a headache.

503 TRUE OR FALSE: Paul loved coconut and could eat as much of it as he liked.

504 In the one-hour "wedding" episode, who did Paul jokingly say "arranged" the frozen vegetable medley that Jamie wanted to throw away?

505 According to Jamie, how does Paul feel about bisque?
   A. He loves it.
   B. He's "uneasy with bisque."
   C. He thinks it's a bread course.
   D. He originally thought it was something for Murray, "like kibble."

506 Where did Jamie eat the big cookie that she said was the best cookie she had ever tasted?

507 What Italian pasta dish did Jamie have to flatten out with a rolling pin when her and Paul's evening alone turned into a dinner party for six?

    A. Fettucine Alfredo

    B. Ravioli with meatballs

    C. Ziti Carbonara

    D. Lasagna

508 In Paul's "Weather Channel" dream, what was he eating when he was sitting on the couch?

    A. Pizza

    B. Potato chips

    C. Chinese food

    D. Lasagna

509 Fran owned an entire book of recipes that focused around one "pepper-like" spice. What was this spice?

    A. Cumin

    B. Dill

    C. Allspice

    D. Tarragon

510 TRUE OR FALSE: Jamie loves tea.

511 What meat course did Jamie order on her and Paul's first date that made him fall in love with her?

    A. Prime rib

    B. Salisbury steak

    C. A veal chop

    D. Pot roast

512 TRUE OR FALSE: Paul was dismayed to learn that instead of pumpkin pie at Thanksgiving, Jamie's family had mince pie.

513 What food items did Paul's mother FedEx to Jamie's parents' house for Thanksgiving dinner?
- A. A turkey and a Jell-O mold
- B. A pumpkin pie and gefilte fish
- C. Kugel and borscht
- D. Oyster stuffing and candied yams

514 What specific pizza topping made Jamie and Paul's across-the-hall neighbors, the Conways, sick?
- A. Sausage
- B. Scrambled eggs
- C. Pineapple
- D. Sardines

515 What famous patriot's shrimp fork was on display in the Museum of Colonial Cutlery that Jamie and Paul saw at the Vermont inn they visited during their "weekend getaway"?
- A. Ben Franklin
- B. Nathan Hale
- C. Thomas Jefferson
- D. Paul Revere

516 TRUE OR FALSE: After the inn where Paul and Jamie stayed in Vermont, the second best place to eat in town was Dobson's Restaurant.

517 Reconstruct the Chinese food order Paul and Jamie placed when they were at the inn in Vermont (and which was actually delivered to the inn from New York City):

    A. Chicken Fried Rice or Shrimp Fried Rice?

    B. General Chao's Chicken or Moo Shoo Pork?

    C. String Beans in Garlic Sauce or Szechuan Vegetables?

    D. Steamed Dumplings or Egg Rolls?

518 TRUE OR FALSE: Paul's mother once got food poisoning from fish she ate at his and Jamie's place.

519 According to Jamie, which of the following antacid tablets contained "precious nutrients"?

    A. Rolaids

    B. Tums

    C. Maalox

520 FILL IN THE BLANK: Even though there was more to Fran and Mark's breakup than a simple food purchase, the catalyst was Mark's purchase of a seven dollar crock of _____ .

521 At work, what was Paul's favorite soup for lunch?

    A. Mushroom barley

    B. Split pea

    C. Tomato

    D. Chicken noodle

522 Why didn't Paul like Eggs Florentine?

    A. Because the name reminded him too much of flu-
oride.

    B. Because his mother made them for breakfast
every Saturday morning when he was a kid.

    C. Because of the spinach.

    D. Because the eggs always came too runny.

523 TRUE OR FALSE: Goober's at *Moby!* cost $4.50 a box.

524 How did Paul once embarrass Jamie when they went
out to dinner at the Spanish restaurant El Greco?

    A. He asked for American cheese on his Quesedilla.

    B. He asked to meet the chef, who was actually a
nineteen-year-old high school kid named Larry.

    C. He forgot his credit card and didn't have enough
cash to pay the bill.

    D. He tried to order in Spanish.

525 Paul and Jamie seemed to have a large quantity of a
certain type of canned vegetable in their cabinet. What
was it?

    A. Creamed corn

    B. Peas

    C. String beans

    D. Beets

526 TRUE OR FALSE: Jamie was an expert omelet maker who
never had to scrap one because of "folding" problems.

527 What breakfast cereal did Jamie once use in a recipe for lasagna?

    A. Rice Krispies

    B. Wheaties

    C. Rice Chex

528 When Paul and Jamie baby-sat for Paul's nephew Jed, Jed told them that his mother always let him eat a certain dairy product as a snack. Jamie didn't believe him. What was this dairy product?

529 Paul once tried to bluff Jamie about allspice, telling her it contained every spice except one. What, according to him, was missing from allspice?

    A. Cumin

    B. Oregano

    C. Basil

    D. Paprika

530 Complete Lou's somewhat revolting remark to Fran: "In ten ounces of meat, there's _____ ounces of blood."

531 While trying to decide between "the chicken and the trout," Paul once revealed (tongue-in-cheek) the title of his favorite childhood story. What was it?

532 What dish did Jamie prepare from scratch for dinner the night she believed Paul was going to propose to her?

    A. Lasagna

    B. Turkey

    C. Rosemary chicken

533 TRUE OR FALSE: Diane "Spy Girl" Caldwell grew her own tarragon.

534 After the trip to the outlet center during which Jamie "acquired" the Blouse of Death, Paul, Jamie, Fran, and Ira ate at the Chinese Bowl. Match the dish with its appropriate title from their meal.

A. Shrimp   1. Of Majesty and Wonder
B. Chicken   2. Happy Delight
C. Bean Curd   3. Wonderful Taste

535 What spice did Ira's mother put "on everything"? ("There was never an incident.")

A. Red pepper
B. MSG
C. Cumin

536 FILL IN THE BLANKS: Paul and Jamie's "tea inventory" included Kiss Today _____ Mint; Hooray for _____ ; and Atomic _____ .

537 Which of the following frozen dinners did Roy Osterback (the guy who ended up with Paul and Jamie's amateur porno tape) have in his freezer?

A. Turkey
B. Veal
C. Salisbury steak
D. All of the above

538 FILL IN THE BLANK: Jamie's cafeteria lunch on her first day back to school was fish sticks and _____ .

539 TRUE OR FALSE: John Astin once invited the Buchmans for a goose dinner.

540 What fruit was Alan Brady particularly fond of giving as a present?
  A. Kumquat
  B. Guava
  C. Pineapple

541 The clam restaurant on the Jersey shore was NOT called Stefano's, Roberto's, Vito's, Boyd's, Eduardo's, Pepe's, Lupé's, or Freddy's. What *was* the name of the place?

542 Why didn't Paul like Trout Almondine?
  A. Because it had bones.
  B. Because he couldn't hear the word "trout" without thinking of "grout."
  C. Because he didn't trust any dish that ended in an "ine."

543 After Jamie and Paul learned that the clam restaurant in Jersey had moved to their block, they ordered two dinners, calamari and clams. Who ordered what?

544 Once when everyone went out to dinner, Paul and Jamie's mothers fought over a certain seafood dish of which there was only one left. What was it?
  A. Lobster
  B. Shrimp scampi
  C. Clams casino

545 What did Paul's mother Sylvia bring as a snack to the movie *Choclat Noye Bechenye?* (HINT: She made Paul eat this fruit instead of his Milk Duds.)

    A. Bananas

    B. Raisins

    C. Grapes

546 Uncle Van really liked a certain type of beef dish. After Van died, Paul accidentally dropped a piece of what meat into Van's ashes urn?

    A. Cubed steak

    B. Salisbury steak

    C. Pork butt

547 When Mr. Wicker moved in with the Buchmans after a fight with his wife, he made them cocoa with a certain spice in it. Name this condiment.

    A. Cinnamon

    B. Allspice

    C. Nutmeg

548 During his extended "visit," Mr. Wicker also made the Buchmans what flaky baked desert?

    A. Popovers

    B. Cupcakes

    C. Croissants

549 FILL IN THE BLANK: The first time Paul and Jamie had everyone at their place for Thanksgiving dinner, they had to get up at _____ A.M. to put the turkey in the oven.

550 What vegetable did Jamie prepare especially for Fran the first time she and Paul had everyone at their apartment for Thanksgiving dinner?

    A. Creamed corn

    B. Brussels sprouts

    C. Peas with bacon bits and little pearl onions

    D. Candied yams

551 TRUE OR FALSE: Ira loved Jamie's meatloaf.

552 What vegetable dish did Paul's mother bring to Paul and Jamie's place for Thanksgiving dinner?

    A. Potatoes

    B. Creamed corn

    C. Broccoli with cheese sauce

553 Paul and Jamie ended up finally needing *five* turkeys for their first Thanksgiving dinner party. From the following list, match the turkey with its ultimate disposition:

    1. Turkey no. 1   A. Stolen in the hallway.

    2. Turkey no. 2   B. Dropped into an alley.

    3. Turkey no. 3   C. Successfully eaten.

    4. Turkey no. 4   D. Eaten by Murray.

    5. Turkey no. 5   E. Thrown out the living room window.

554 TRUE OR FALSE: Paul slurps his soup.

555 What was Paul and Jamie's "usual" order at Riff's?

    A. A cheeseburger and a chef salad

    B. A tossed salad and curly fries

    C. A hamburger and potato skins

556 TRUE OR FALSE: Paul was very careful about resealing the bagel bag.

557 The night Paul and Jamie went out with Ira and Velma, Paul stepped on a piece of meat that was on the sidewalk. What cut of meat did he get on his shoe?

   A. Pork
   B. Salisbury steak
   C. Veal

558 At Fran's party at which Paul insulted an NBC executive, what was wrong with her guacamole?

   A. It needed lemon.
   B. Not enough green chili.
   C. Too much red pepper.

559 Lisa frustrated Jamie by telling her that she ate her job interviewer's breakfast during the interview. What did she take off the guy's desk and eat?

   A. A bagel
   B. A donut
   C. A Danish

For Seriously *Mad* Fans

560 What enormous emotional trauma caused Fran to one day find herself at D'Agostino's "eating Mallomars and swigging a Bud Light"? (HINT: Think "Mark!")

561 What did Paul's father say every time he dropped ice into a drink?

   A. "Plop, plop, fizz, fizz."
   B. "Splink, splink."
   C. "Ice ta know ya!"

562 According to Paul, what juice was "as much fun to say as it is to drink"?

    A. Papaya

    B. Mango

    C. Guava

16

Guest Stars

Paul, Jamie, and "virtual reality" fantasy girl, Christie Brinkley.

This chapter tests your knowledge of some rather well-known visitors who played a part in Paul and Jamie's lives.

563 Who rented Paul's old bachelor apartment until Paul gave up the lease?

564 Lisa Kudrow, who plays Ursula the waitress, once appeared on *Mad About You* as a blind date named Karen for Paul. Where did Karen make her appearance?

    A. Central Park

    B. Rockefeller Plaza skating rink

    C. Riff's

    D. Central Perk

565 What did Freddy Statler (played by Jerry Lewis) respond when Paul asked him, "Why do you want a film?"

    A. "To show to my LAAAAAAADY!"

    B. "Because a statue takes too long!"

    C. "Because I love to say 'sprockets' in mixed company!"

566 Which of the following Beatles collectibles did Freddy Statler buy for Paul?

    A. Paul's bass

    B. George's guitar

    C. John's harmonica

    D. Ringo's drums

567 Freddy Statler bought a painting from the Pope for Jamie. Name the artist.

    A. Monet

    B. Da Vinci

    C. Picasso

    D. Rembrandt

568 What famous Italian tenor gave a private performance in Paul and Jamie's apartment, thanks to Freddy Statler?

569 It was revealed in the episode "The Spy Who Loved Me" that Diane "Spy Girl" Caldwell (played by Barbara Feldon) almost got a sitcom role that ultimately went to Marlo Thomas. What role did Diane lose?

570 In the episode "The Man Who Said Hello," who replaced Kathie Lee Gifford on *Live With Regis and Kathie Lee*?

571 Supply the last names of the other guests on *Live With Regis and Kathie Lee* the day Burt Buchman was on the show:

    A. Marvin &rule;

    B. Claudia &rule;

    C. Daniel &rule;

572 Which of Paul's coworkers described himself by telling Fran, "I'm a peripheral visionary. I can see into the future but just way off to the side"?

573 What word did Christie Brinkley mistakenly tell Paul was "such a lonely word"?

574 What famous rock widow invited Paul and Jamie to a party at her apartment?
- A. Courtney Love
- B. Yoko Ono
- C. Rita Marley

575 What *Today Show* star reported on the Jamie-induced New York City blackout?
- A. Bryant Gumbel
- B. Katie Couric
- C. Al Roker
- D. Willard Scott

576 John Astin played an eccentric guy who moved into Paul and Jamie's building. For what famous television character was Astin best known?
- A. Uncle Martin on *My Favorite Martian*
- B. Gomez Addams on *The Addams Family*
- C. Herman Munster on *The Munsters*
- D. Fonzie on *Happy Days*

577 What was John Astin's motto?
- A. "Back flips never hurt anyone!"
- B. "Never eat standing what you can eat sitting down!"
- C. "Jackets for everyone!"
- D. "Neighbors are always trouble!"

578 What New York City mayor defended the Big Apple in the tag to the episode in which Paul and Jamie have a series of disastrous experiences in one night out on the town?

    A. Ed Koch

    B. Rudolph Giuliani

579 What popular actor played Jamie's ex-boyfriend Alan, the guy with whom she had a running argument about who broke up with whom?

    A. Brad Pitt

    B. Johnny Depp

    C. Eric Stoltz

580 What famous supermodel appeared in both Paul and Murray's dreams? (HINT: Think Rod Stewart and *The Tonight Show*)

    A. Vendela

    B. Rachel Hunter

    C. Cindy Crawford

581 In a special episode of *Friends*, Jamie and Fran visited Central Perk and met Ursula's twin sister, Phoebe. What did Fran and Jamie order in the coffeehouse?

    A. Two caffe lattes and some Biscotti cookies

    B. Two espressos and one croissant

    C. Two American coffees and an apple Danish

17

(PHOTOFEST)

Paul Reiser
and Helen Hunt

Here are a few questions about the lives and careers of the talented actors who make our beloved Paul and Jamie come alive.

Paul Reiser "Resume Review" Questions

582 In what television series did Paul Reiser star with Greg Evigan before he moved on to *Mad About You*?

    A. *B. J. and the Bear*
    B. *Masquerade*
    C. *A Year at the Top*
    D. *My Two Dads*

583 In addition to *Mad About You*, Paul Reiser also has a successful feature film career. From the following list of his films, match the movie with his costar:

A. *Cross My Heart*	1. Eddie Murphy
B. *Diner*	2. Sigourney Weaver
C. *Beverly Hills Cop*	3. Daryl Hannah
D. *Aliens*	4. Kim Basinger
E. *Crazy People*	5. Annette O'Toole
F. *Bye Bye, Love*	6. Joe Mantegna
G. *The Marrying Man*	7. Randy Quaid
H. *Family Prayers*	8. Ellen Barkin

584 Paul replied, "Only the first one," when Mark once asked him, "Did you ever see that movie _____?" What three-movie series was Mark asking Paul *Buchman* about?

585 Identify the quote that Paul Reiser initially used to pitch *Mad About You* to the executives at NBC:
- A. "It's like *The Dick Van Dyke Show* but with sex and a dog."
- B. "It's *thirtysomething*, only shorter and funnier."
- C. "It's like a married *Seinfeld*, but without a Kramer."
- D. It's like *Bewitched*, but without the magic or the alcoholics."

586 What is the title of Paul Reiser's best-selling book?
- A. *Bing, Bang, Boom*
- B. *Love and Marriage*
- C. *Couplehood*
- D. *Seinlanguage*

Helen Hunt "Resume Review" Questions

587 In the episode "Love Among the Tiles," Paul and Jamie get trapped in their bathroom on Valentine's Day. As they eat antacids, Paul remarks, "It's like *Swiss Family Robinson*." What does this insider reference have to do with Helen Hunt?

588 In addition to *Mad About You*, Helen Hunt also has a successful feature film career. From the following list of her films, match the movie with her costar:

A. *Girls Just Want to Have Fun*
B. *Into the Badlands*
C. *Miles From Home*
D. *Mr. Saturday Night*
E. *Peggy Sue Got Married*
F. *Project X*
G. *Stealing Home*
H. *Trancers*
I. *The Waterdance*
J. *Kiss of Death*

1. Richard Gere
2. Kathleen Turner
3. Jodie Foster
4. Eric Stoltz
5. Sarah Jessica Parker
6. Tim Thomerson
7. Matthew Broderick
8. David Caruso
9. Dylan McDermott
10. Billy Crystal

589 What popular television medical series did Helen Hunt have a recurring role on before *Mad About You*?

A. *Marcus Welby, M.D.*
B. *The Doctors*
C. *St. Elsewhere*

18

Ad-libs, Bloopers, Teases, Tags, and Outtakes

◀

How was Murray supposed to know the turkey wasn't for him? He is after all part of the family, right?

This chapter has some fun with the openings and closings ("teases" and "tags") of episodes; as well as a few ad-libs, outtakes, and boo-boos.

590 In the episode "Togetherness," Paul says to Jamie, "We don't have a fire escape." What, as the saying goes, is wrong with this picture?

591 During one episode's tag, Paul Reiser cracks up Helen Hunt with an ad-lib about her getting a "Movie of the Week." What game were "Paul and Jamie" *supposed* to be playing?

    A. Pictionary

    B. Monopoly

    C. Trivial Pursuit

"She brings so much of herself to the show. An issue we've dealt with is kids—do we or don't we want them? And there was a line Jamie said on the show [about my nephew] and I went, 'Jeez, type that up.'"

—Paul Reiser, in *Us* magazine

---

592 Complete the following Helen Hunt ad-lib, which was said in the episode in which Paul and Jamie took his nephew Jed trick or treating: "Your nephew is so sweet, my _____ hurts."

593 In the tag to the "Jerry Lewis" episode ("The Billionaire"), an outtake is shown of Jerry trying to pronounce a certain name. Whose name did he mangle?

594 In the tag to the Atlantic City episode, a handsome gentleman offers Paul $1 million to sleep with Jamie, an offer which they both eagerly accept. What movie did this scene parody?

595 In the tag to the episode "It's a Wrap," Paul dictates over the phone to Lou the show's closing credits. Fill in the blanks of Paul's instructions: "Show the guy on the _____ ; then the sound of the _____ ; do the thing with the hand and then the stupid _____ with wings."

596 In the tag to the episode in which Fran is worried she's pregnant, one cast member asks the others why she wasn't in the episode. Who was it?

597 Who was Paul *Reiser* talking about when he said (in the tag to the "virtual reality" episode), "*Helen*, let her play!"?

598 In the tag to the episode in which Jamie's thirtieth birthday plans go awry, the Suave Singers perform an *a cappella* version of a song that Paul pretended he couldn't recognize at first, but then did, once they sang the chorus. What song did they sing and what does this have to do with Paul Reiser?

599 In the tag to the episode "The Last Scampi," Paul Reiser and Helen Hunt tell the viewers that Murray's mother was played by Murray's *real* mother. Who then calls into the scene and asks Helen Hunt if she wrote this episode?

600 In the episode in which Paul tries to figure out how to "pick up" Jamie, he tries a pickup line on her that acknowledges Helen Hunt's astonishing resemblance to a certain Academy Award-winning actress. What did Paul ask her?

601 In the tease to the episode in which Paul and Jamie go on vacation as his parents, Jamie tries to get out of walking Murray by reciting for Paul, in correct order, the names of what celestial bodies?

The *Mad About You* Character Word Search Puzzle

The following clues will help you find the words in the *Mad About You* Word Search puzzle. (The word in **BOLD** is the one you need to look for in the puzzle.)

Paul's dad, **BURT** Buchman

Fran **DEVANOW**, Jamie's former boss

DUTCH, the clerk at the Video Village

EDDIE the doorman

"As we jump into the final **FRONTIER**"

Jamie's father, **GUS** Stemple

IRA Buchman, Paul's beloved cousin

JAMIE Buchman, PR wizard

KIM, the owner of the mini-mart

Ira's casino-manager wife, Marianne **LUGASO**

MANNY Gantz, Jamie's boss

MARK Devanow, divorcé, OB/GYN, and wayfarer

MURRAY the dog

Mad About You's home network, **NBC**

PAUL Buchman, filmmaker

Fran and Mark's son, **RYAN**

SELBY, Paul's former college roommate

Paul's older sister, **SHARON**

SOPHIE, the Conways' dog

Lisa **STEMPLE**, Jamie's sister

Paul's mom, **SYLVIA** Buchman

Jamie's mother, **THERESA** Stemple

URSULA, the waitress at Riff's

Paul's editor and cameraman, **WARREN** Mermelman

The Buchmans' super, Bill **WICKER**

```
S  M  A  I  A  L  Q  T  W  A  S  S  U  G  D
E  O  U  S  R  L  N  B  C  N  A  C  K  U  C
M  D  P  R  E  F  U  T  O  Z  Z  G  T  Z  I
L  A  D  H  R  R  R  S  R  T  U  C  C  B  A
K  C  N  I  I  A  E  O  R  E  H  E  D  R  H
O  A  K  N  E  E  Y  H  N  U  K  E  S  D  T
B  T  I  W  Y  C  Y  F  T  T  V  C  D  O  P
V  Y  M  I  I  R  R  J  A  A  I  L  I  V  L
A  Y  K  H  A  V  A  V  N  E  U  E  A  W  U
R  B  H  D  D  M  N  O  L  G  N  I  R  Z  A
I  N  Y  B  I  E  W  P  A  O  V  Y  A  L  P
K  A  L  E  R  Q  M  S  R  L  B  S  Q  T  T
R  Y  C  R  D  E  O  A  Y  L  N  Q  T  O  R
A  R  A  M  T  E  H  S  E  N  J  R  E  F  U
M  W  E  S  Y  S  I  S  T  G  D  Q  L  E  B
```

BURT	LUGASO	SHARON
DEVANOW	MANNY	SOPHIE
DUTCH	MARK	STEMPLE
EDDIE	MURRAY	SYLVIA
FRONTIER	NBC	THERESA
GUS	PAUL	URSULA
IRA	RYAN	WARREN
JAMIE	SELBY	WICKER
KIM		

Answers

1. *Mad About You:* The Basics

1 D.

2 C.

3 TRUE.

4 D.

5 E.

6 TRUE.

7 B.

8 A,2; B,1.

9 C.

10 B and D.

11 TRUE.

12 "I do okay; I'm renting; Nope; Nope; Nope."

13 In her office during a Christmas party.

14 A.

15 D.

16 Sharon; Debbie.

17 A.

18 A.

19 TRUE.

20 B.

21 B.

22 C.

23 C. (She lived across the street from Paul and yet they didn't know each other!)

24 Because Jamie Stemple Buchman was also born and raised in New Haven. (And no, unfortunately I never knew her growing up!)

25 When they first met at a newsstand, Jamie told Paul that her parents' obituaries were in the last *New York Times* in order to get the paper, and on the train to New Haven, she told the woman sitting in the seat Paul wanted that they were on their way to the funeral of Paul's mother in order to get her to give up the seat.

2. JAMIE AND PAUL BUCHMAN

26 A.

27 TRUE.

28 A.

29 TRUE.

30 A.

31 Eunice? (Jamie originally told Paul her middle name was Karen, but then she blurted out that it was Eunice during the fifteen-minute documentary. When Paul asked her about it, she replied, "I lied." Was she lying about "Karen" or "Eunice"? It's your call.)

32 B.

33 B.

34 A.

35 TRUE. ("Don't assume!")

36 C.

37 Ethics; Psychology; Logic; Intermediate French.

38 D. (André Agassi's, of course.)

39 B.

40 D.

41 C.

42 B.

43 TRUE.

44 B.

45 B.

46 TRUE.

47 C.

48 TRUE.

49 C.

50 TRUE. (She blurted this out during the "fifteen-minute documentary" episode but it was never discussed further or shown.)

51 C.

52 D.

53 2:01 A.M.

54 A.

55 B.

56 FALSE. He did not own a car.

57 D.

58 FALSE. He could not ride backwards.

59 C.

60 TRUE. But he did put it on when he went to meet Lynne Stoddard, whom he (mistakenly) believed had once been his girlfriend.

61 C.

62 TRUE. (Selby wasn't impressed. He said *everything* rhymed with "Lynne.")

63 He was neatly stacking his change on the bureau before going to bed.

64 TRUE.

65 C.

66 Hannibal Lecter.

67 D.

68 FALSE. He hates it. (He thought it "loud, long, and boring.")

69 FALSE. He liked his shower "firm, but not pelting."

70 B.

71 They got bright red.

72 TRUE.

73 A.

74 TRUE.

75 C.

76 *Irene.*

77 According to Paul, they disappeared.

78 TRUE.

79 B.

80 TRUE.

81 B.

82 TRUE.

83 FALSE. Actually, the exact *opposite* is closer to the truth.

84 He said he'd be a Good Humor Man. (He liked the little square truck with the doors, the bell, and the change-maker.)

85 TRUE.

86 TRUE (according to Jamie).

87 The right side (looking down on the bed).

88 A.

89 C.

90 A.

91 C. (He lamented he didn't know anything from *Brigadoon.*)

92 A.

93 D.

94 B.

95 A.

96 Paul felt that Jamie always used too much floss.

97 "registration."

98 Twice. First, in the pilot episode, "Romantic Improvisations," and then in the first season finale episode, "Happy Anniversary."

99 B.

100 A.

101 They were at the wake of the *other* Paul Buchman.

102 A.

103 B.

104 From Yoko Ono.

105 B.

106 A.

107 He said, "I'm kissing your knees."

108 FALSE. They first met (fatefully, according to Jamie) as children twenty years earlier during a blackout at the Museum of Natural History.

3. THE APARTMENT

109 C.

110 The apartment had a "slanty" floor.

111 TRUE.

112 A.

113 A.

114 C.

115 The blender and blow dryer; the toaster and popcorn maker.

116 B.

117 TRUE.

118 C.

119 B.

120 38 inches.

121 C.

122 C.

123 The Conways.

124 Lou.

125 TRUE.

126 B.

127 D.

128 A.

129 This was Jamie's derogatory nickname for their neighbors across the hall, the Conways.

130 D.

131 FALSE. Their landlord was Mel Wurtzel (Mr. Wicker was their super.)

132 FALSE. They live in Lower Manhattan.

133 D.

134 A.

135 TRUE.

136 TRUE.

137 D.

138 TRUE.

139 1,E; 2,A; 3,B; 4,C; 5,D.

140 TRUE.

141 C.

4. A MAD ABOUT YOU MISCELLANY

142 Fran; Fran; Jamie; Jamie; Fran; Jamie.

143 1,E; 2,A; 3,D; 4,B; 5,C.

144 B.

145 C.

146 "Corruption"; "Ruination"

147 Paul; Ira; Ira; Paul; Paul; Ira.

148 TRUE. ("It's in the book!")

149 A.

150 C.

151 D.

152 FALSE. He was going to see *Cats*.

153 A.

154 FALSE. She still had Paul's *Three Dog Night* albums.

155 B. (He identified one of his own songs.)

156 B.

157 D.

158 "Easy-listening."

159 A.

160 TRUE.

161 C.

162 D.

163 A.

164 Hal Wallis. (Jamie graciously allowed Paul to tell her this piece of film trivia over and over.)

165 TRUE. (He loved to dance on his knees during the gang scene.)

166 *The Pope of Greenwich Village.*

167 A.

168 C.

169 B.

170 A.

171 C.

172 C.

173 A.

174 D. (The September 1975 issue.)

175 B.

176 B.

177 C.

178 B.

179 C.

180 Paul, in his and Jamie's last-resort, Aruba, role-playing sex fantasy.

181 Paul and Jamie.

182 Paul and Jamie. These are the incorrect names Diane "Spy Girl" Caldwell insisted on calling the Buchmans.

183 This was Paul's name for Jamie, because she never seemed to need to pee.

184 Jamie, after Paul accidentally pumped her full of four cups of caffeine-rich Atomic Zinger tea.

185 Paul and Ira after working out.

186 Paul, when he had to wear Lisa's mittens after she lost his "Yukon gloves."

187 C This is what Paul called her after she got mad at him for not giving her advance notice about their fifteen-minute documentary.

188 Jamie. This is how she described herself after realizing that she had been in the corporate world for years.

189 R.

190 C.

191 B.

192 The kid, named Edward Wagner (an homagé to science fiction author Karl Edward Wagner, perhaps?), was fourteen, and taught at Columbia.

193 A.

194 TRUE.

195 422.

196 C.

197 A.

198 "Bob Howard."

199 He put them in the freezer for a while and then made her put them on.

200 A.

201 B.

202 B.

203 FALSE: He played Nintendo Gameboy.

204 C.

205 A: Lisa; B: Jamie; C: Lisa; D: Lisa; E: Jamie; F: Lisa; G: Lisa; H: Lisa; I: Lisa; J: Lisa; K: Lisa; L: Lisa; M: Jamie; N: Jamie; O: Jamie; P: Jamie; Q: Lisa; R: Lisa; S: Lisa; T: Lisa; U: Lisa.

206 Jamie, to the Teamsters who worked for her on her commercial shoots.

5. LISA

207 C.

208 TRUE. During Paul's fifteen-minute documentary, Lisa changed her sweater in front of him—oncamera.

209 B.

210 FALSE. It actually took her five years to graduate.

211 B.

212 Harriet.

213 TRUE.
214 B.
215 FALSE. She lives in a fifth floor apartment.
216 D.
217 FALSE. She only attended three years.
218 C. She decided that if Will Rogers ever met her, he wouldn't like her.
219 FALSE. He was married.
220 TRUE.
221 C.
222 Strange, but TRUE.
223 A, 2; B,3; C,1.
224 TRUE.
225 "teeth"; "French"; "French."
226 B.
227 "Nowhere."
228 Liam Neeson.
229 A.
230 C.
231 TRUE.
232 B.
233 TRUE.
234 A.
235 TRUE.
236 C.
237 A.
238 He was her mailman.
239 South Dakota.
240 B.
241 Fran and Ira.
242 C.
243 B.
244 B. ("Let them try and check!")
245 Betsy.
246 TRUE.

247 C.
248 B.
249 TRUE.
250 A.
251 She used to put them on her nipples.
252 TRUE.
253 B.

6. IRA

254 FALSE. He first appears in the episode "The Wedding Affair." His band played the wedding and Paul and Jamie were invited guests.
255 A and C.
256 C.
257 A.
258 TRUE.
259 C.
260 TRUE.
261 Paul.
262 B.
263 C.
264 A.
265 B.
266 E. Paul ordered them all because they were "comp" guests of Ira's "wife" Marianne Lugaso.
267 Plastic.
268 B.
269 TRUE.
270 A.
271 C.
272 B.
273 C.
274 A.
275 B.

276 TRUE.

277 C.

278 A.

279 Velma made all of these claims except for H.

280 A.

281 B.

282 FALSE. They bathed together exactly twice in their entire life.

283 B.

7. MURRAY

284 D.

285 FALSE. He's a collie-mix.

286 TRUE.

287 D.

288 D.

289 TRUE. Ira gave Murray Paul's turkey sandwich.

290 TRUE.

291 A.

292 B. It means feeling unwell or unhappy.

293 Poodles.

294 Murray was, ahem, "cleaning" himself.

295 "rug."

296 A box in which Paul and Jamie kept things from Murray's life, including his dog school diploma and his first collar.

297 A.

298 C.

299 He was standing perfectly still on top of their dining room table.

300 Five: four boys and one girl.

301 C.

302 B.

303 C.

304 Seven.

305 A.

8. FRAN AND MARK DEVANOW

306 TRUE. He unwittingly walked in on her when she was taking a shower at their apartment.

307 FALSE. She liked being on top.

308 A.

309 Ira.

310 B.

311 FALSE. Fran not only went to a gym on a regular basis, but she also often jogged to Paul and Jamie's place from her apartment on the upper West Side.

312 D.

313 A.

314 A.

315 B.

316 Charades.

317 A.

318 FALSE. Fran proposed to Mark.

319 Mark's hangnail.

320 A.

321 D.

322 David.

323 TRUE.

324 C.

325 TRUE.

326 A.

327 YES.

328 "Antonio" is the name Mark used to work as a busboy in a diner in New York City.

329 D.

330 TRUE.

331 A,4; B,6; C,2; D,1; E,5; G,7.

332 A.

333 YES.

334 A.

335 Paul told him the Muffin Man was dead.

336 B.

337 They were both named Murray.

338 TRUE.

339 B.

340 1925.

9. PARENTS AND RELATIVES

341 B.

342 FALSE. He liked French's mustard.

343 C.

344 TRUE.

345 A.

346 TRUE. She appeared five times (once as "Pretty Girl No. 3") on *The Alan Brady Show*.

347 D.

348 C.

349 Uncle Jules.

350 Twenty-six hours.

351 TRUE.

352 A.

353 C.

354 A.

355 A.

356 B.

357 TRUE.

358 A.

359 B.

360 A.

361 TRUE.

362 A.

363 B.

10. URSULA

364 TRUE.

365 B. Ursula's twin sister Phoebe on *Friends* is a masseuse.

366 TRUE. (It was in the tag to the episode "Destructive Criticism.")

367 A.

368 Two. She cut up Paul and Jamie's Visa cards.

369 No, but Ira told Paul he though he got Ursula pregnant to get out of telling him that he thought he had gotten *Fran* pregnant.

370 FALSE. Ursula never *could* remember to whom she lent her mittens.

371 A.

372 Phoebe.

373 At Central Perk, in the series *Friends*.

11. SELBY

374 TRUE.

375 C.

376 TRUE.

377 YES. Selby tortured Paul with her, trying to persuade him to double date with him.

378 A.

379 C.

380 FALSE. His complete name was Jay Selby, but like Kramer on *Seinfeld*, Norton on *The Honeymooners*, and Carter on *ER*, he was almost always addressed only by his last name.

12. MADLY QUOTABLE

381 "Second happiest."

382 "Royally."

383 Jamie's.

384 Their parents.

385 "They installed them."

386 A.

387 She thought it would make him feel better after he got upset that Mark had been her gynecologist and had examined her (in the *stirrups*).

388 Her "devil child" Ryan. (Paul replied, "I was thwarting? Right there I was thwarting?")

389 A.

390 Paul, at the Christmas party at Jamie's office.

391 TRUE.

392 Paul.

393 A.

394 B.

395 Paul. She was referring to her maid Masha's unrequited love for Paul.

396 "Yippee!"

397 Recycling.

398 "Not Annette! A net!" (This exchange took place when Lisa defended her irresponsible ways to Jamie ["I leap!"], who responded that she then ended up running all over New York with a net.)

399 Lisa. (He had just bounced a book off her head.)

400 Who else? His cameraman extraordinaire, Warren (Eddie) Mermelman.

401 That extremely odd couple, Warren and Connie.

402 Delivering triplets. (After hearing this, Lisa remarked, "Makes *me* want to have children.")

403 Paul, after seeing a baby picture of himself that accompanied an article about his father, "The Man Who Said Hello."

404 C.

405 A.

406 Paul and Jamie. (They were spending the night in Paul's old bedroom when Burt was in the hospital.)

407 Paul. (He was talking about him and Jamie.)

408 The Three Stooges. (Paul, needless to say, did not agree.)

409 Lisa, who else? (Jamie replied, "What's not to like?")

410 Ira, to Jamie.

411 His "producer" Lou Bonaparte, who cut out a montage from one of Paul's documentaries without asking him.

412 Again, who else? Lisa.

413 Paul. (She was responding to his lecherous selection of Christie Brinkley as his "virtual reality" fantasy partner.)

414 Girls.

415 A,3; B,4; C,1; D,2 (but Paul made this one up).

416 "skyline."

417 Some kind of fluid on the earpiece of a New York City pay phone.

418 "It's banana."

419 "mothers."

420 His wife, Maggie. She mumbled.

421 He was talking *to* the Conways, but he was talking *about* the English.

422 C.

423 A.

424 C.

425 "gland."

426 Giving a muffin to the guy who tried to steal his and Jamie's cab.

427 Lesbian scenes in X-rated movies.

428 Milton Berle is rumored to be enormously, ahem, "endowed."

429 A.

430 C.

13. WORK

431 B.

432 C.

433 A.
434 FALSE. He was Brady's editor for twelve years.
435 A.
436 *The Andy Griffith Show.*
437 A.
438 B.
439 B.
440 B.
441 C.
442 B.
443 D.
444 *New York at Night.*
445 C.
446 They are all "Chicago people": people Paul worked with for the two months he shot a film in the Windy City.
447 C.
448 A. "Seatbelt," B. "Seatbelts," C. "Seatbelt," D. "Seatbelts."
449 Six.
450 A.
451 B.
452 C.
453 C.
454 B.
455 A.
456 B.
457 D.
458 B.
459 C.
460 B. (She sang the national anthem.)
461 B.
462 TRUE.
463 C.
464 TRUE.
465 C.

466 B.

467 TRUE.

468 Gantz.

469 A.

470 D. (Do you think it might have had something to do with throwing turkeys out of highrise windows?!)

471 A.

472 A.

473 TRUE.

474 TRUE.

475 A.

476 E.

477 TRUE.

478 "Home."

479 A.

480 Fran, who had had the job in the first place.

481 B.

482 A.

483 C.

484 B.

485 No. She was from Minsk.

486 C.

487 B.

488 C.

489 C.

14. CLOTHING AND JEWELRY

490 A picture of Paul's face in the center of a bullseye.

491 Bikini underwear.

492 Paul, when she first met him.

493 B.

494 TRUE.

495 D.

---

496 B.
497 Plaid.
498 C.
499 Fran got it "below cost" from Mark's uncle.
500 B.
501 Flowers; candy; earrings; a brooch; a bracelet; a peignoir.

15. Food

502 FALSE. She loves chocolates.
503 FALSE. Paul was allergic to coconut.
504 Henry Mancini.
505 B.
506 At the furniture store.
507 D.
508 B.
509 A.
510 FALSE. She hates it.
511 C.
512 TRUE.
513 A.
514 C.
515 D.
516 TRUE.
517 Chicken Fried Rice, Moo Shoo Pork, Szechuan Vegetables, and Steamed Dumplings.
518 TRUE.
519 B.
520 Mustard.
521 A.
522 C.
523 TRUE.
524 D.
525 B.

526 FALSE. One time she ruined three omelets and worked one and a half hours to get one to fold correctly.

527 A.

528 Butter.

529 D.

530 "two."

531 "The Chicken and the Trout"

532 C. (She forgot to turn on the oven and it ended up "chicken tartare.")

533 TRUE. ("It's in the book!")

534 A,2 ("Happy Delight Shrimp"); B,3 ("Wonderful Taste Chicken"); C,1 ("Bean Curd of Majesty and Wonder").

535 B.

536 "Goodbye"; "Lemons"; "Zinger."

537 D.

538 Sprite.

539 TRUE.

540 C.

541 Clamenza!

542 A.

543 Paul had the calamari; Jamie had the clams.

544 B.

545 C.

546 B.

547 C.

548 A.

549 5:25.

550 B.

551 TRUE.

552 A.

553 1,D; 2,A; 3,E; 4,B; 5,C.

554 TRUE.

555 A.

556 FALSE. He usually ripped it open and didn't worry about closing it. Jamie, on the other hand, was *very* careful about reclosing the bag carefully.

557 C.

558 A.

559 C.

560 She did this after Mark's leaving her finally "hit her."

561 B.

562 C.

16. Guest Stars

563 The *Seinfeld* show's Cosmo Kramer, played by Michael Richards.

564 C.

565 B.

566 D. (Warren remarked, "Now they'll never get back together again.")

567 B.

568 Luciano Pavarotti.

569 She was almost going to be *That Girl*.

570 Regis's wife, Joy Philbin.

571 Hamlisch; Cohen; Day-Lewis.

572 Warren Mermelman.

573 "Honestly." (This was a reference to the classic song "Honesty" by her then-husband Billy Joel.)

574 B.

575 C.

576 B.

577 C.

578 B.

579 C.

580 B.

581 A.

17. PAUL REISER AND HELEN HUNT

582 D.

583 A,5; B,8; C,1; D,2; E,3; F,7; G,4; H,6.

584 The *Alien* series. (Paul Reiser starred in the second installment of the series.)

585 B.

586 C.

587 From 1975 through 1976 (at the age of twelve), Helen Hunt starred as Helga Wagner in the television series *Swiss Family Robinson*.

588 A,5; B,9; C,1; D,10; E,2; F,7; G,3; H,6; I,4; J,8.

589 C.

18. AD-LIBS, BLOOPERS, TEASES, TAGS, AND OUTTAKES

590 In several subsequent episodes, not only is a fire escape seen, it actually figures into plot lines (Murray and Sophie; Paul home early from Chicago hiding from his mother, etc.).

591 B.

592 "uterus."

593 He tried unsuccessfully to pronounce Warren's last name "Mermelman."

594 *Indecent Proposal*, with Robert Redford and Demi Moore.

595 "phone"; "racetrack"; "horse."

596 Anne "Lisa Stemple" Ramsay.

597 Christie Brinkley, who was pretending to be Paul *Buchman*'s wife.

598 They sang the theme to *Mad About You*, "Final Frontier," which was written by Paul Reiser and Don Was.

599 Paul Reiser's real mother, whom Helen Hunt addresses as "Mrs. Reiser."

600 "Anybody ever tell you you look like Jodie Foster?"

601 The planets in the Solar System. (At first she misses Neptune, and then she misses Jupiter.)

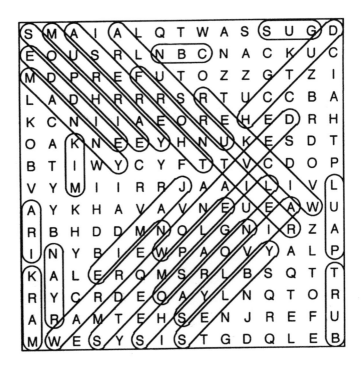

BURT	LUGASO	SHARON
DEVANOW	MANNY	SOPHIE
DUTCH	MARK	STEMPLE
EDDIE	MURRAY	SYLVIA
FRONTIER	NBC	THERESA
GUS	PAUL	URSULA
IRA	RYAN	WARREN
JAMIE	SELBY	WICKER
KIM		

EXTRAS

MAD ABOUT YOU'S CAST OF CHARACTERS

Main Characters

Paul Buchman — Paul Reiser

Jamie Buchman — Helen Hunt

Lisa Stemple, Jamie's sister — Anne Ramsay

Ira Buchman, Paul's cousin — John Pankow

Fran Devanow, Jamie's best friend — Leila Kenzle

Mark Devanow, Fran's husband — Richard Kind

Murray, Paul and Jamie's dog — Maui

Sylvia Buchman, Paul's mother — Cynthia Harris

Theresa Stemple, Jamie's mother — Nancy Dussault (1st) / Penny Fuller (2nd)

Burt Buchman, Paul's father — Louis Zorich

Gus Stemple, Jamie's father — Paul Dooley (1st) / John Karlen (2nd)

Warren Mermelman, Paul's editor/cameraman — Steven Wright

Jay Selby, Paul's friend — Tommy Hinkley

Lou Bonaparte, Paul's producer — Larry Miller

Ike, Paul's editor — Art Evans

Stacey, Paul's assistant — Kerri Green

Connie, Paul's assistant — Meagan Fay

Remy, Paul's assistant — Marva Hicks

Ryan Devanow, Fran and Mark's son — Spencer Klein

Sharon, Paul's sister — Randy Graff

What's Your *Mad About You* I.Q?

Debbie, Paul's sister	Talia Balsam (1st)
	Robin Bartlett (2nd)
Ursula, waitress at Riff's	Lisa Kudrow
Bill Wicker, the Buchmans' super	Jerry Adler
Maggie Conway, the Buchmans' neighbor	Judy Geeson
Hal Conway, Maggie's husband	Paxton Whitehead (1st)
	Jim Piddock (2nd)
Kim, the grocer	Darrell Kunitomi (1st)
	Ping Wu (2nd)
Jed, Debbie's son	Bradley Pierce
Noah, Debbie's son	Andrew J. Ferchland

Supporting Characters

Aunt Lolly	Meg Wyllie
Masha the Maid	Beata Pozniak
Sid, Paul's editor	George D. Petrie
Ricky, Jamie's assistant	Cameron Thor
Manny Gantz	Wayne Tippitt (1st)
	Jack Shearer (2nd)
Roy Osterback	Perry Anzilotti
Dutch	Steve Paymer
Mel Wertzel, the Buchmans' landlord	Louis Goss
Uncle Jules, Paul's uncle	Al Ruscio
Eddie, the Buchmans' doorman	Lou Cutell
Susannah, Ira's girlfriend	Anne Bobby

Famous Guest Stars

Freddy Statler, the Billionaire	Jerry Lewis
Diane Caldwell, "Spy Girl"	Barbara Feldon

Marianne Lugaso, Ira's wife	Cyndi Lauper
Albert Urbont	Allan Arbus
French Professor	Julia Sweeney
Claire Wicker	Anita Gillette
Alan, Jamie's ex-boyfriend	Eric Stoltz
Carol, the NBC miniseries executive	Wendie Malick
Howie Balenger	Steve Buscemi
Kramer	Michael Richards
Sherman Williams	Rick Rossovich
Sloopy Dunbar	Charles Hallahan
Sergeant Panino	Jerry Adler
Vacky the Vendor	Phil Leeds

Celebrity Guest Stars

André Agassi	Himself
John Astin	Himself
Christie Brinkley	Herself
Garth Brooks	Himself
Patrick Ewing	Himself
Rudolph Giuliani	Himself
Regis and Joy Philbin	Themselves
Al Roker	Himself

MAD ABOUT YOU: THE EPISODES

First Season	Air Date
1. "Romantic Improvisations" [Premiere]	9/23/92
2. "Sofa's Choice"	9/30/92
3. "Sunday Times"	10/7/92
4. "Out of the Past"	10/14/92
5. "Paul in the Family"	10/21/92
6. "I'm Just So Happy for You"	10/28/92
7. "Token Friend"	11/4/92
8. "The Apartment"	11/11/92
9. "Riding Backwards"	11/18/92
10. "Neighbors From Hell"	11/25/92
11. "Met Someone"	12/16/92
12. "Maid About You"	1/6/93
13. "Togetherness"	1/13/93
14. "Weekend Getaway"	1/27/93
15. "The Wedding Affair"	2/6/93
16. "Love Among the Tiles"	2/13/93
17. "The Billionaire"	2/20/93
18. "The Man Who Said Hello"	2/27/93
19. "Swept Away"	4/30/93
20. "The Spy Who Loved Me"	5/8/93
21. "The Painter"	5/15/93
22. "Happy Anniversary" [Season Finale]	5/22/93

Second Season	Air Date
1. "Murray's Tale"	9/16/93
2. "Bing Bang Boom"	9/23/93

3.	"Bedfellows"	9/30/93
4.	"Married to the Job"	10/7/93
5.	"So I Married a Hair Murderer"	10/14/93
6.	"The Unplanned Child"	10/28/93
7.	"Natural History"	11/4/93
8.	"Surprise"	11/11/93
9.	"A Pair of Hearts"	11/18/93
10.	"It's a Wrap"	12/2/93
11.	"Destructive Criticism"	12/9/93
12.	"Paul Is Dead"	1/6/94
13.	"Same Time Next Week"	1/13/94
14.	"The Late Show"	1/27/94
15.	"Virtual Reality"	2/3/94
16.	"Cold Feet"	2/10/94
17.	"Instant Karma"	2/14/94
18.	"The Tape"	2/24/94
19.	"Love Letters"	3/10/94
20.	"The Last Scampi"	4/7/94
21.	"Disorientation"	4/28/94
22.	"Storms We Cannot Weather"	5/5/94
23.	"Up All Night"	5/12/94
24.	"With This Ring" [One-hour Season Finale]	5/19/93

Third Season   Air Date

1.	"Escape From New York"	9/22/94
2.	"Home"	9/29/94
3.	"Till Death Do Us Part"	10/6/94
4.	"When I'm Sixty-Four"	10/13/94
5.	"Legacy"	10/20/94
6.	"Pandora's Box"	11/3/94
7.	"The Ride Home"	11/10/94
8.	"Giblets for Murray"	11/17/94
9.	"Once More, With Feeling"	12/8/94
10.	"The City"	12/15/94

11.	"Our Fifteen Minutes"	1/5/95
12.	"How to Fall in Love"	1/19/95
13.	"Mad About You" [One-hour]	2/2/95
14.	"Just My Dog"	2/9/95
15.	"The Alan Brady Show"	2/16/95
16.	"Mad Without You"	2/23/95
17.	"Purseona"	3/9/95
18.	"Two Tickets To Paradise"	3/30/95
19.	"Money Changes Everything"	4/27/95
20.	"Cake Fear"	5/4/95
21.	"My Boyfriend's Back!"	5/11/95
22.	"Up in Smoke" [One-hour Season Finale]	5/18/95

An Obscure *Mad About You* Factoid You Can Use to Dazzle and Impress Your Friends

At the conclusion of each *Mad About You* episode, the name of Paul Reiser's production company, NUANCE PRODUCTIONS, appears in the credits.

The question is, where did Paul Reiser come up with a name like "Nuance Productions" anyway?

Here is one possible answer to that question:

Paul Reiser made his film debut in 1982 in Barry Levinson's wonderful comedy-drama, *Diner*. He played a fifties guy named Modell and his first speaking scene took place in a car driven by Mickey Rourke.

Now I know that *Diner* is supposed to have been "Written and Directed by Barry Levinson," but as a knowledgeable Paul Reiser/*Mad About You* fan, you tell me if the following speech, the first words spoken in the film by Paul Reiser as Modell, sound familiar (he's talking to Mickey Rourke):

*You know what word I'm not comfortable with? "Nuance."
It's not a real word, like "gesture." "Gesture" is a good
word. At least you know where you stand with "gesture."
But "nuance?" I don't know. Maybe I'm wrong.*

I don't know. Maybe I'm wrong. But that rant sounds like a Paul Buchman riff from Word One.

And to bolster my case, "gesture" has also been a word of weight in a *Mad About You* episode as well.

Now go wow your friends with your astonishingly exhaustive knowledge of television history.

You're welcome.

ABOUT THE AUTHOR

STEPHEN J. SPIGNESI is a writer who specializes in popular culture subjects, including television, film, and contemporary fiction. His other books include:

- *Mayberry, My Hometown* (Popular Culture, Ink.)
- *The Complete Stephen King Encyclopedia* (Contemporary Books)
- *The Stephen King Quiz Book* (Signet)
- *The Second Stephen King Quiz Book* (Signet)
- *The Woody Allen Companion* (Andrews and McNeel)
- *The Official "Gone With the Wind" Companion* (Plume)
- *The V.C. Andrews Trivia and Quiz Book* (Signet)
- *The Odd Index* (Plume)
- *The Gore Galore Video Quiz Book* (Signet)
- *The Celebrity Baby Name Book* (Signet)

In addition to writing, Spignesi also lectures widely on a variety of popular culture subjects and is the founder of the small press publishing company, The Stephen John Press. He lives in New Haven with his wife Pam.

More Entertaining Facts and Trivia

After the Funeral: The Posthumous Adventures of Famous Corpses by Edwin Murphy $9.95 paper #51599

The Almanac of Fascinating Beginnings: From the Academy Awards to the Xerox Machine by Norman King $9.95 paper #51549

Born This Day: A Daily Celebration of Famous Beginnings by Ed Morrow $10.95 paper #51648

The "Cheers" Trivia Book by Mark Wenger $ 9.95 paper #51482

The Citadel Treasury of Famous Movie Lines by Ted Gottfried $ 21.95 paper #51551

The "Christmas Carol" Trivia Book: Everything You Ever Wanted to Know ABout Every Version of the Dickens Classic by Paul Sammon $ 8.95 paper #51579

The Critics Were Wrong: The 501 Most Misguided Movie Reviews by Ardis Sillick & Michael McCormick $9.95 paper #51722

The Cutting Room Floor: Movie Scenes Which Never Made It to the Movies by Laurent Bouzereau $14.95 paper #51491

Death by Rock & Roll: The Untimely Deaths of the Legends of Rock by Gary J. Katz $9.95 paper #51581

Did She or Didn't She?: Behind the Bedroom Doors of 201 Famous Women by Mart Martin $9.95 paper #51669

Film Flubs: Memorable Movie Mistakes by Bill Givens $7.95 paper #51161
Also available:
Son of Film Flubs: More Memorable Movie Mistakes by Bill Givens $7.95 paper #51279
Film Flubs: The Sequel - Even More Memorable Movie Mistakes by Bill Givens $7.95 paper #51360

Final Curtain: Deaths of Noted Movie and TV Personalities by Everett G. Jarvist $17.95 paper #51646

The "Seinfeld" Aptitude Test: Hundreds of Spectacular Questions on Minute Details from TV's Greatest Show About Absolutely Nothing by Beth B. Golub $8.95 paper #51583

701 Toughest Movie Trivia Questions of All Time by William Macadams & Paul Nelson $9.95 paper #51700

Shot on This Site: A Traveler's Guide to the Places and Locations Used to Film Famous Movies and Television Show by William A. Gordon $14.95 paper #51647

Sophomore Slumps: Disastrous Second Movies, Albums, Songs and TV Shows by Chris Golden $9.95 paper #51584

The Star Fleet Academy Entrance Exam: Tantalizing Trivia From Classic *Star Trek* to *Star Trek: Voyager* by Peggy Robin $9.95 paper #51695

The Star Trek Concordance: The A-to-Z Guide to the Classic Original Television Series and Films by Bjo Trimble $19.95 paper #51610

1201 Toughest TV Trivia Questions of All Time by Vincent Terrace $9.95 paper #51730

The Ultimate John Wayne Trivia Book by Alvin H. Marill $8.95 paper #51660

What's Your "Frasier" IQ?: 501 Questions and Answers for Fans by Robert Bly $8.95 paper #51732

What's Your "Mad About You" IQ?: 601 Questions and Answers for Fans by Stephen Spignesi $8.95 paper #51682

The Woman's Book of Movie Quotes; compiled by Jeff Bloch $9.95 paper #51629

The Worst Movies of All Time: Or, What Were They Thinking? by Michael Sauter $14.95 paper #51577